Colloquium
on
Crime

Colloquium on Crime

Eleven Renowned Mystery Writers Discuss Their Work

Robin W. Winks

EDITOR

CHARLES SCRIBNER'S SONS
New York

Contents

Colloquium
on
Crime

Introduction

This collection of eleven essays is intended to tell us why writers of mystery and detective fiction write as they do. The essays are partly autobiographical, partly critical, and entirely enjoyable, for they reveal far more about some of our best writers than can be gleaned from the back flap of a dust jacket. Taken together, the essays are intended as an exploration into the nature of mystery fiction.

The genesis of the collection was quite simple. As a reviewer of detective fiction, I comment on perhaps seventy books a year. To find seventy about which I have something to say, I read perhaps three times as many. By now I know who I like best and have some inkling of why, and I decided to write to my fifteen favorite living authors (wouldn't work otherwise, would it, mate?) and put to them some questions. It turned out that four of my favorites didn't like being interrogated this way, and so they are not here, but eleven of those writers found it amusing, perhaps even productive, to think about themselves, their work habits, and the words they use as authors. These eleven essays, very lightly edited—

these are professionals, after all, and they do not require an amateur, much less a critic, messing in—are the result of this guileless approach.

Who are my favorite writers of mystery fiction and why? As to who, most of them are here. Over the years I have discovered how to tell a favorite without undue worry for literary theory: a writer I will buy in hard cover rather than waiting for paperback. All of these are hardcover writers in my definition (though, given the nature of the genre, many of them have published books which appeared first, or only, in paper). I do not leave books by these writers behind in airplane seats, loan them to friends, or donate them to libraries, all foolproof ways to get rid of books that otherwise will crowd up one's shelves.

Even so, why these eleven? Because they all do supremely well those tasks—not tasks, really, more like fun—I associate with the best in mystery fiction. First, they entertain. They are professionals who take their writing very seriously (for example, they meet deadlines, one sure sign of a professional) because they live by it and for it. They may bootleg to the reader much perfectly accurate and fascinating ethnology, as Tony Hillerman does through the eyes of his Navajo Tribal Policemen, Jim Chee and Joe Leaphorn, but they do not forget to entertain. They may, by virtue of the environment they describe, tell us much about the subtle interchange between the races under apartheid, as James McClure does with his South African series, but they let the reader decide on his own attitudes toward what he has seen. Some, like Joseph Hansen, are subtly social critics, for one cannot read of Hansen's Brandstetter without a changed sense of how the gay world must view the straight. But first, they entertain.

They also instruct. Because they entertain first, they may then instruct, a lesson long learned by good teachers. Five of the authors were, in fact, academics, and two retain their teaching positions; others were in journalism, science, the law—all instructive forms of discourse. Thus these writers

2

know how to ask the right questions, how to pose a problem (and knowing, how to confuse the issue), how to lay out by path straight or crooked an answer. Some instruct us in how people speak: there is no finer ear for the demotic vulgarity of working-class life in America than K. C. Constantine's. The first eighty pages of his most recent book, *Upon Some Midnights Clear*, ought to be studied in every linguistics class in the country. Some instruct us in ambiguity and irony in the toughest of ways: there can be few books so disturbing to our sense of moral balance as Rex Burns's *Angle of Attack*. Some show us how to create a plot so tight, the pages turn of themselves even when there is no breeze: Donald Hamilton.

Of course, each reader finds different pleasures, different instruction in mystery fiction. I do not read such fiction for escape and I dislike the term; it degrades the reader. I read for engagement, to oil up the engine so that I can sit down to my own work. There is nothing like a good detective novel, or a short, superbly crafted poem, to put one in the mood to get back to that monograph on the evolution of barbed wire (on the Nebraska frontier, 1888 to 1902, with special reference to the Sand Hills Country). So too, I think, do most readers of such fiction (I omit here those who read books written to formulae, to a length specified by the publisher, or about damsels in distress: just as I have a list of favorite writers, I have a list of fifteen least favorite as well).

Readers of mystery fiction read to turn the engine on, not off. I continue to wonder why so intelligent a review medium as the *New York Times Book Review* feels that its mystery columns must be illustrated with asthmatic-looking men and women of no discernible intelligence rooted to their seats, eyes popping, mouths agape, as though such a reaction were typical either of the kind of reader such fiction attracts or of the fiction itself. This is serious fiction. Because it is serious, it is entertaining.

I look for three elements above all in good mystery fiction.

3

First, the book must read well. The author must show that
he or she cares about how the language is used. Ask any of
the writers in this book who their favorite author is, and the
reply is almost always someone who wrote truly well, whether
A. A. Milne or Charles Dickens or Jane Austen. Second, I
look for a strong sense of place. Theft, murder, rape happen
in a place; often the details of that place promote or obscure
the crime, sometimes the crime arises from that place. I want
my author to know what he is talking about, not to get his
French-Canadian locutions wrong and his Geneva dockside
bass-ackwards, as one best-selling author did in another of
his huge survey of disinformation a few years ago. Getting
the scene and the language right is important, because it
shows respect for the reader and because motivated crime
(we set aside the sociopaths for the moment) occurs in a
context. When Reginald Hill wrote of a working-class English rugger club in *A Clubbable Woman*, it mattered that the
sport was rugby, not tennis, and that Hill knew the rules of
the game.

And then, of course, there is the historian in me: good
detective fiction proceeds very much according to the meth-
odology of the historian. To take one example only, in history, that most democratic of disciplines, every fact must count
equally at the beginning of an inquiry, for one may not pre-
judge the conclusion. In the end, some facts will matter more
than others, some will account more satisfactorily for the
chain of cause and effect that one is tracing. But not at the
beginning: to decide at the outset which facts matter most is
to write history as a participant, not as an observer, and what
participant ever got all his sums right? To decide at the outset
who did it—the middle class, the Fascists, Aaron Burr, the
Enola Gay—and why, and What It All Means, is to destroy
the democratic principles of historical inquiry. The fictional
detective—one doubts this is invariably true of every detective down at the local precinct house—must also credit each

fact with the same weight at the outset. The police procedural is not far from the historian's procedure.

Others will enjoy detective fiction for other reasons, their own reasons. They will like the way Spenser throws away his one-liners in Robert Parker's *A Catskill Eagle*. They will enjoy the quiet, steady, accumulative sense of expertise that suffuses everything Michael Gilbert does. They will like the satire, for satirist he is, of Robert Barnard, and the clear-eyed vision of how evil may be done without violence, of which Dorothy Salisbury Davis is so good at reminding us. I like all this, too, but every author in this collection is here for my own three reasons: because each author writes well, each is honest to a sense of place, each may instruct through entertaining.

Though each writer is quite individual, there are certain elements in common among the essays, and these elements arise in part because of the questions I put to the authors. Two or three authors make it clear they found those questions a bit silly, or too academic, and quite possibly they were. Questions that interest me include the trite (Why does a person begin to write crime fiction?), the intrusive (How much of yourself do you put into what you write? What earlier authors do you see as most influencing your sense of style?), the mildly didactic (Where do you see the genre going? Is it inherently conservative? Is the current academic discovery of crime fiction, usually embedded in the idea of "popular culture," a good thing?). The questions were all obvious ones, for there was nary a Barthes or Derrida among them, and I did have the wisdom to tell my chosen lot to put to themselves any questions they wanted to answer and to go to it. Thus some essays speak to each other and some do not, for I thought it artificial to ask X whether he liked Y, who was also appearing in the book, even when Z made it perfectly clear that by omitting A (whom I cannot abide), I had lost all credibility as editor or critic.

A reader might ask, who are the four authors among my

fifteen favorites who are not here? I won't answer that question, though I will say that had those four been present, the balance between American and English writers would have been as exact as an odd number could make it, and that the same would be true between the genders, though I did not set out to achieve either affirmative action or another gesture of hands-across-the-sea. There are good writers on the Continent, of course, and in Canada, Australia, Africa, India. But I do not, yet, buy them in hard cover.

When asked what a writer must do to survive, James Joyce replied that he must practice secrecy, silence, and cunning. So precisely might the writers who have engaged in this colloquium have responded. The twelve of us agree, I think, that the best work in mystery fiction is, in the end, based on the greatest mystery of all: human character. Through these writers we meet all of humanity. What could be more instructive? Better yet, what could be more entertaining?

Robin W. Winks

ROBIN W. WINKS is the Randolph W. Townsend, Jr., Professor of History and Master of Berkeley College at Yale University. He teaches the history of race relations and of comparative imperialisms; his avocation is mystery and detective fiction, and he has written three books on the subject: *The Historian as Detective, Detective Fiction*, and *Modus Operandi*. His monthly review column, which began in *The New Republic* some years ago, now appears in the *Boston Globe*.

Growing Up to Crime

Robert Barnard

Round about the age of twelve or thirteen I graduated to adult reading, passing directly from the works of Enid Blyton to the works of Agatha Christie. Both writers, I realize in retrospect, are warned against for the poverty of their vocabularies and the suspect nature of their racial attitudes. I hope that in both respects I have remained unscathed. But when librarians try to ban the former, and when historians of crime fiction denigrate the latter, I suspect that what is really operating is that old-fashioned, puritan suspicion of entertainment, which is so difficult for the Anglo-Saxon to throw off. Both write unashamedly to give pleasure, to beguile. To win the plaudits of their detractors they would have to enclose in the sugar of their entertainments a pill of social consciousness or one of in-depth psychological analysis.

Thus, my prejudice in favor of detective stories as entertainment (a prejudice I have written about elsewhere, and which I won't go on about here) is long-standing and deep-rooted, and I distrust people who try to take the detective story in other directions. I like my crime stories to be well written, but that is a marginal pleasure compared to the pleasure of their being well plotted, fast, ingenious. I do not want the genre to attain a borderline literary respectability. The writers who are used to argue the respectability of the form (it used to be Dorothy L. Sayers, then it was Raymond Chandler, nowadays it seems to be Dashiell Hammett) are those I regard with a high degree of suspicion. *The Glass Key* seems to me one of the dullest and deadest books I have ever, from a silly sense of duty, struggled to the end of, and the symbol of the Maltese falcon among the most contrived and unconvincing in literature. How pathetic the alcohol-soaked cries of American hard-boiled writers for serious recognition! How humiliating Chandler's groveling gratitude when he was adopted by the shop-soiled British literary establishment! As usual, Agatha Christie got it exactly right: "One is a craftsman." Let us not get ideas above our station, or we may miss the train altogether.

When I had discovered Christie, I read, with the voraciousness of adolescence, others of her ilk: Marsh, Allingham, Brand, and back to Doyle. I don't remember reading Sayers, so perhaps I tried and was put off by the heaviness, the snobbery, or the anti-Semitism. Certainly I have had to work hard to enjoy her in maturity. I think my reactions to these writers then was not substantially different from my reactions now. When one reads writers *on* Doyle, with their talk about the wonderful atmosphere of late-Victorian London, of hansom cabs splashing through the gaslit streets, and so on, one rather expects layers of "fine writing"—perhaps of the kind that Raymond Chandler so frequently assured his correspondents he was good at. Nothing of the sort. Doyle is hard, factual, informative, and the whole is saved from dryness by the wonderful ingenuity of his mind, and the spice and humor of the central duo. Marsh seemed to me a great and lively talent, but marred by her dreary and repetitive determination to establish precisely where everyone was at the stroke of 2:42. Allingham, on the other hand, was an especial favorite: high-spirited, free-wheeling, a loving celebrant of English eccentricity and English villainy. Even Allingham, though, lost me in those books (mostly from the late thirties) when she seemed to be aiming at the approval of serious critics, and in fact she was always an uneven writer, producing some decidedly dull books among the classics. For these reasons, I would have put these two writers a rung or two below Christie. She—this was in the early fifties—was so damned *reliable*! I still feel that way, and still feel that Christie's prolificity and consistency put her in a class of her own.

Shortly afterward I discovered *Wuthering Heights*, and then Dickens, and thus wandered off onto the broad highway of English literature. I went to university, and then taught literature to Australians and Norwegians. For some years this took all my energies, and seemed to be worthwhile.

At this point (and only at the insistence of the General Editor of this book) I will attempt to answer questions I am often asked: why Australia? Why Norway? I do not usually answer these, because the truth is so boring, and the questioner probably imagines some mysterious, Conradesque reason, or sees my travels as at least *mildly* swashbuckling, in an academic kind of way.

The truth is that I went to these places entirely by accident. After university I worked for a year for the Fabian Society, a conservatively socialistic society dedicated to right thinking and good doing. I left it when the British Council informed me that I had got a job at the University of Mandalay which they were recruiting for. Three days before I was due to sail, they wrote saying "Sorry, old chap, the appointment wasn't confirmed. Bye-bye." I have loathed the British Council and all its doings from that time. I was then unemployed for three months, and got a job in the small-town University of New England, in New South Wales, partly through contacts (the editor who accepted my first article, Norman Jeffares, had ties with Australia), partly because it was only that sort of university that would accept anyone as unqualified as I.

Why did I want to leave Britain, even to the extent of being willing to go to Mandalay, the road to which I had no Kiplingesque longings to tread? I don't think it was from any distaste for the country, merely the need to have experienced something else *as well*. It was easier, in those days, to travel the world and find employment here, there, and everywhere. Frontiers and barriers have loomed much larger since.

Again, when after five years at Armidale my wife, who is Australian, was pressing very strongly (you know how it is) to leave the place and go to Europe, there were not many universities willing to employ someone as largely unqualified as I still was. Bergen advertised, I applied, and got the job as their second choice. When we were informed, we had to go and look up Bergen on the map. It happened to be Norway, but it could equally have been Portugal—in which case I would no doubt have written *Death in a Warm* and not a *Cold Climate*. When we first went there, Bergen was one of the loveliest cities in Europe (since ruined by the motor car and inept planning). I took a doctorate on Dickens (why Dickens? asks the General Editor, which is like asking a musical person why he likes Beethoven, and is similarly unanswerable), and in 1976 I moved up to Arctic climes and midnight sun to become professor in Tromsø.

Was I teaching in order to gain bread while I learned how to write? Certainly not consciously in those years. I wanted to teach at university because I knew I was hopeless at teaching in an ordinary school (I was incapable of maintaining discipline—though I think I might manage now). It was, or seemed, an end in itself. I was certainly not conscious of any gift for writing, let alone any impulse to write. I think one reason I felt the need for a supplementary interest in university teaching may lie in the Norwegian education system.

It is rigid and inadequate, and seems designed to discourage children from reading. I don't think in my entire seventeen years in the country I met more than five or six Norwegians who read constantly, voraciously, for pleasure. In the end it becomes dispiriting teaching students who invariably judge a book by the number of its pages, and equally invariably fail to get to the end.

My adult life has been a chapter of accidents, most of them, so far, happy. I suspect that this is the case for all but a very few, chosen spirits. Saints and great statesmen make themselves what they are, but clergymen and politicians get to be that way by a series of muddly accidents.

There—that was boring, wasn't it? Let's get on.

My first attempt at writing fiction was begun round about 1968, when I had been teaching for seven years and felt I had the job under my belt. The attempt foundered at Chapter Three. The first chapter was, I think, pretty funny: it centered on the voyage to Australia of a fearsome Tory female politician, who was modeled on Mrs. Thatcher. This was truly prescient, I feel, since the lady was at the time only opposition spokesman on education. I rather pride myself on my nose for human awfulness. Once I had got her and her hopeless son to Australia, the thing began to meander downhill and I realized that serious fiction, even comic serious fiction, needed some kind of plot and purpose, and that I had very little talent in that direction. You could say I came to crime fiction as some kind of refugee: the traditional whodunit had the rudimentary outlines of the plot ready-made. Sooner or later the reader had to be provided with a body, and the subsequent sections of the book had to be devoted to elucidating the hows and whys of the killing. Around these standard requirements, involving very little narrative inventiveness on my part, I could weave a story that also called on some of the things I thought I was rather better at: humor, characterization, and so on.

In passing, I would say that I do rather regret the necessity for the body. One of the many reasons for admiring Conan Doyle, and for placing him on the pinnacle, is the variety of his crimes and misdemeanors, which in themselves seem to tell us so much about the Victorians, their values and habits. The only time I have departed from the formulaic body, I have done so for the base reason that I wanted to stop my American publisher from changing my titles to horribly flat ones beginning *Death of a....* In any event they called the bodiless one *The Case of....* Game and match to them, especially as it wasn't a very good book. The problem remains: how to retain the interest of the modern reader without the stimulant of blood. It *can* be done, but I suspect that only Ruth Rendell, of our present-day practitioners, has the sort of imagination that might show us how it is to be accomplished.

When I turned to crime, I started off on the wrong foot, with a serious story set in Norway, and involving ex-collaborators with the Quisling regime, and looted art treasures. Luckily it was rejected, but luckily too it was just good enough for the first publisher I sent it to to send back a long, reasoned letter of rejection (how I loathe publishers—and it seems to be practically all of them, these days—who send back form letters of refusal, of no use at all to aspirant writers). This letter, from the lady who was to become my first, only, and much-valued English editor, also asked to have first look at any future manuscripts. Hence, on that modicum of encouragement, and interrupted only by the writing of a doctorate, I embarked joyfully on a quite different kind of detective story, to which I eventually gave the good but misleading title of *Death of an Old Goat.*

I should emphasize that even then I had no expectation of publication. I suppose only someone very naive or absurdly full of themselves actually *expects* their first works to be published. If I had, I would probably have softened the tone of the book considerably: it is, even for me, decidedly bilious. It does not even represent my real feelings about Australia, where the book is set; it merely crystallizes the feelings I had about the country during my first few months there, and exaggerates them for comic effect. I can't regret this now, because it does make for a dark, sardonic book which seems to strike a chord in many breasts that have been exiled, whether briefly or permanently, in that vast, empty tract. And the whole does capture, I think, some of the atmosphere of the hick university town in the mountains where it is set, and where I spent my five Australian years: proudly mediocre, and soaked in alcohol from the early hours of the day (the town, I mean, not me).

The book's plot was something of an improvisation, I am afraid. I knew from the beginning who was to be murdered: it was the aged visiting professor. (The book owed something to the visit to Armidale of Professor Mario Praz—not to the *person*, for I never met him, merely to the occasion—and to his lecture on "Dostoevsky and Colin Wilson," an example of life being much more absurd than anything one can get away with in literature.) I knew from the start that the last sentence of the book had to contain a clinching surprise. I hadn't read the great Margaret Millar then, so this determination must have sprung from a feeling that the revelation of the murderer in a mystery usually leaves too much pedestrian tying-up-of-the-ends afterward. Beyond that, I fear I just launched into the writing, and hoped that ideas would occur to me. I remember being quite unsure of the significance of the word "scout" long after the word was used in the crucial scene just before the murder—though I was quite sure that it did have to be significant. An improviser, alas, I remain, with a pathetic trust that everything will somehow come right by page one hundred and eighty-nine. I now find that if I do work out a plot, with clueing, well in advance of writing, this constricts and irritates me, and much of the zest goes out of the writing.

The acceptance of this by the editor of Collins Crime Club (Christie and Marsh's publishers, an inevitable first choice) meant that from now on I was committed to crime, and to crime with a comic slant. My relationship with Collins has suffered the odd hiccup: there was my second book, set in the year 2000-odd, with the present queen, a distinctly Lady Bracknellish figure, finding her heirs and successors being knocked off one by one—rejected, I always thought, because Sir William Collins was hoping for a Life Peerage. Then there was *The Resurrection Men*, a blasphemous novella giving an account of what really went on between the first Good Friday and the first Ascension Day—rejected, I feel, because Collins are the official English publishers of the Bible, and they didn't want to put an alternative (and much funnier) version into circulation. But broadly speaking we have been very happy together, as I have, later, with Scribners in the States, and the broad commitment to crime-with-comedy has never been in question, up to the present.

Since the English style of murder mystery does not wallow in blood and gore—is, in fact, something of an abstract exercise—there is considerable scope for comedy there. This potential is largely left untapped by Christie and Marsh—or, rather, they left the humor very much beneath the surface of the text. It *is* there, as some of the performances in the Christie films (notably Ingrid Bergman in *Orient Express* and Angela Lansbury in *Nile*) bear witness to. On the other hand, there was Allingham with the glorious Lugg, there was Christianna Brand, there was *Bullet in the Ballet*, there was Joyce Porter's irresistible *Dover One*. This last, I suspect, had been behind my thuggish Australian policeman in *Old Goat* (no, let me be completely honest: I know it was; I cribbed him). My books over the years have almost all been humorous in intention: darkly so in *Mother's Boys*, more boisterous in *Political Suicide*. They are all more or less ironic in style, and they are populated by grotesques. The exception is *Out of the Blackout,* which I loved writing because the idea had grabbed me so irresistibly, though as it turned out I had considerable difficulty in finding an appropriate style for it. No doubt I shall return to the serious vein now and again in the future. Unremitting irony can get as tiresome for the writer as for the reader.

I do not apologize for the caricature nature of almost all my characterizations. Caricature is the basis of the humorous novel, from Fielding to early Waugh. Quite often I have stolen my pale shadows from those great masters, and in *Unruly Son* I cribbed the central figure from Waugh himself. The playwright Joe Orton's mother, as described in John Lahr's *Prick Up Your Ears,* was the spark that ignited *Mother's Boys* (one of my favorite books, though my English editor dearly wanted to reject it on the grounds that matricide was not only repulsive—it simply didn't happen). The Sitwells and the Mitfords lie behind, though a good way behind, *Sheer Torture.* It will be seen that in life, as in literature, I like and admire grotesques and eccentrics, and listen avidly on buses and trains (no true writer ought willingly to travel by car) for conversations that reveal new depths of oddity or sheer dreadfulness.

The advantages of caricatures for the writer of the traditional whodunit are obvious. He has to establish a fair number of suspects, and establish them unequivocally in readers' minds, while leaving much of their natures unrevealed. A few broadly sketched characteristics of person or speech are invaluable. A caricature is essentially a shell, a performance. What is behind it is a mystery; its inner life is the subject of guesswork. A notable critic of Dickens has remarked how horrifying it would be to be admitted to the inner life of Mr. Pecksniff, though acquaintance with the outer shell of the man is consistently delightful. So it should be with potential suspects in a detective story. The moment the writer enters any suspect's thoughts, the alert reader sits up: is he cheating?

Is he being deliberately ambiguous? Is he telling the whole truth? Could a murderer, so soon after his crime, think about *anything* without the murder obtruding? Such thoughts are often rather alienating. Best merely to *suggest* an inner life beneath the carapace of the public personality, and to use those suggestions when the time for a solution arrives.

By now it will be clear that my favorite crime writers are likely to point the needle of their ambitions more toward *The Importance of Being Ernest* than toward *Macbeth*. The form itself is of necessity artificial, and though this artificiality and limitedness may be disguised (as the late Ross Macdonald, for example, so brilliantly disguised the stereotyped nature of his procedures and the narrow range of his preoccupations), my own feeling is that it is more satisfactory to exploit them, cherish them, play new tricks with them. Artificiality is no literary failing, no weakness to be apologized for: we cherish Wilde and Congreve, Peacock and Coward. This does not mean that we should brandish the conventions at the reader, or be openly knowing about the artifice that is part of the genre. That is merely irritating. Once embarked on the form, one should play it for real, just as *The Importance* is funniest when the actors are most serious, and seem to care most deeply how it was that the baby got into the handbag. One of the reasons I dislike the film of *Ten Little Niggers*, the René Clair version which everyone seems to praise these days, is that all the cast acts as if it were one huge joke, and none for a moment act as if they were on an island where murder has occurred, and where the next victims in the series might well be themselves. This is so artificial, the filmmakers seem to be saying, that we can't take it seriously. They should, on the contrary, say: this is so artificial that we *must* take it seriously. Play it for real, write it for real. Do not apologize for the conventions: cherish them and renew them by new twists.

If I am critical in any way of the Golden Age writers of

the British detective story, it is that they let themselves become a little too straight-jacketed in their choice of settings. Because in fact the formula can be applied to any setting under the sun, and embrace any mood or style. Christie's settings were much more varied than is sometimes implied, yet one does feel on occasion that one has had one's fill of the English village. When, quite late in her career, Marsh wrote a book with a country-house party at which all the servants were ex-convicts, it did seem that, for her at least, the genre was on the verge of bankruptcy.

I cannot claim any great originality for the settings of my books, but I have tried not to repeat myself too often. I have now written two with an English village setting, and feel that the time has come to call a halt there. After two or three stately home murders, the same could be said about that setting (though I make no promises, for the opportunities for cultural cross-references and in-jokes are so enormous). I do think it is important, in lighting on a setting, not to let ignorance of the milieu deter one. I do know something of the English village, but I know nothing of the stately home, except on a day-tripper level. The critic whose praise I have cherished above all others is the American one who said, of *Death on the High C's*, that "Mr. Barnard obviously knows the world of backstage opera from A to Z." God bless America for its perceptive critics of crime books (would that Britain had just one or two as perceptive), but it must be said that I have never set toe backstage in an opera house. Nor, for that matter, have I ever been inside a working monastery—the setting for *Blood Brotherhood*. Nor could I draw on any intimate knowledge of royalty for *Death and the Princess*. I have in mind a book set in the publishing offices of a pornographic magazine, though my ignorance of pornography is quite blush-making; eventually I shall write one with a sporting background (why are there so few?), though of sport I know nothing whatsoever. Just as mere proof would not

17

convince the lady in Thurber, so total ignorance will not deter me.

I love that review of *High C's* because it concentrates the mind wonderfully on who it is one has to fool. I did not write *High C's* for opera singers, but for people who might like the illusion of being behind the scenes in an opera company. If I can do a minimum of research and convince the outsider that I know this world, then that is all that is required. Opera singers, I would guess, do not read anything much except their notices and musical notation (and frequently not even the latter), but if one should read my book I'm perfectly aware that he or she would find mistakes— probably highly risible mistakes—on every page. Similarly with monks and royalty (neither of them great readers, fortunately). They are welcome to that warm glow of superiority they will feel at knowing so much more about the subject than the author. I'd even welcome letters from them, telling me all the howlers I have made. As with people who guess the solution before the murder is even committed, it makes *them* feel so warm and smug that it can't be bad for the author. The aim must be, in Gilbert's words that might be the motto for the literary charlatan, to provide "corroborative detail, intended to give artistic verisimilitude to an otherwise bald and unconvincing narrative."

This view has been rather forced upon me, in fact, in that, in the broader sense as well, I have all the time been writing about something of which I have had only a sketchy and dated knowledge. I have lived almost all my adult life in Australia and Norway, and thus I have always been thoroughly out of touch with the country I have supposedly been writing about. This I had left in 1961, at the age of twenty-four. Thus, in a book like *A Little Local Murder*, there are many things from the Britain of the time it was written (1975), but essentially it is a novel about the Britain of my last period of residence there (the late fifties), thus making it a thoroughly schizophrenic book. Visits to a country, even when it is your own, only allow you to skim its surface—that is why those package-tour mysteries such as *When in Rome* (Marsh), *A Caribbean Mystery* (Christie), or *Speaker of Mandarin* (Rendell) are always less than satisfactory. Better to invent your own country, as in Brand's *Tour de Force*. Gradually over the years, I had to ask my editor for so much—from the price of butter to the brands of beer that men in Britain drank—or, more damaging, had to leave so much vague and unconcretized, that eventually it became inevitable that I should move back. Fortunately, by 1983, the Americans were buying my books in such numbers that I could cast from my boots the dust of the groves of Academe, and move "home." At least the British in my books would start talking as British people do today.

But I soon found that it is "home" rather than home. From being a foreigner in Norway, I have returned to become a foreigner in my own country. I have been away so long that I do not have the shared experiences of those who have never left. Perhaps that is not a bad image of the writer—the eternal immigrant, with one foot perpetually inside the country and the other still outside. I often look with interest at the immigrants in British cities who have changed the country so much for the better while I have been away, giving it so much more vitality, variety, and "edge," and wonder when they will produce a crime writer who will open up their culture to those of us outside.

So I stand, still on the edge of the community, watching and listening, and cataloguing changes. I feel, I suppose, much as the Empire-builders felt in earlier times when they came back to their chilly retirements in Bournemouth or Torquay. Sometimes, still further alienated, I seem to be looking at an entirely foreign country with the fascinated eyes of a Pissarro or a Doré. What manner of place is this, what people are these? But I hope in the books to come that the picture of Britain will be more specific, more felt, more convincing. I hope, too, that it will open up areas that crime writers have seldom ventured into. For we have, have we not, been restricted in our social range? Even those crime writers who have reacted most against the snobberies of Sayers, Marsh, et al. have very seldom strayed outside the class area that can be defined as educated middle class. Indeed, there are vast social tracts—for example, the young couples on housing estates, with vast mortgages—that no novelist of any kind in Britain seems to want to deal with. A corpse may be as good a way as any of opening those areas up. There are still pathetically few crime novels that deal with the working class from the inside—not the world of the semicriminal slums, but the working working class, in dreary jobs, in fear of unemployment, living on council estates, and enjoying fish and chips and beer. They entered the English novel with *Sons and Lovers*, reentered it triumphantly in the fifties, but somehow the detective story, as so often, has lagged decades behind. The working class are no longer in crime books as objects of ridicule or fear. They are hardly there at all.

I seem to be straying dangerously close to the question "Whither the Crime Novel?," which is not, to my mind, a very fruitful line of inquiry. It is the sort of question journalists put to more or less distinguished people, to be answered in a more or less informed fashion, but what emerges seldom does more than fill up a page or two for them. And in the case of a popular fiction form, the answer to the question "Where is it going?" is probably that it doesn't *go* anywhere: it *is*. Popular interest in intriguing crime goes back to the pamphlets on Sir Edmund Godfrey's murder, to More and Bacon on the princes in the tower, and doubtless way beyond. Hammett adds the private eye to the thieves' world literature that had produced *Jonathan Wild*, *Moll Flanders*, and the Elizabethan "coney-catching" journalism. Chandler put a fuzzy glow around the private eye, as in a not-too-good

Victorian painting of Christ or King Arthur. Hammett gave murder back to the people who commit it; Ross Macdonald took it away from them again. On the whole the changes are small, the enduring characteristics wide and basic. Raymond Chandler is a lot closer to Agatha Christie than he is to Hemingway or Scott Fitzgerald, for all his ambitions.

So the only safe thing to predict about the crime novel in the future is that it will not essentially alter. On the other hand, this element or that element will certainly gain or lose prominence—that's how it has always been. I would hope to see a downward orientation class-wise, but I doubt if it will happen. Depressions demand glamor and excitement, and one thing we can say about the eighties is that they are likely to remain depressed.

So what this essay has come down to—sorry about that—is little more than a statement of likes and dislikes. I dislike (or, to be more accurate, I have in me a built-in resistance to) the American hard-boiled novel, because it presents a world inhabited exclusively by men of violence and shoddy moral standards. I cannot be interested in the violence perpetrated by men of violence, as it seems to matter little which of the various men of violence perpetrated it. But I know that the hard-boiled school touches a nerve in many, and of course it will go on—is doing so, in the distinguished hands of Parker, Vallin, and many more. Similarly, I am a mite distrustful (most ungratefully distrustful, in view of the many hours of pleasure her books have given me) of the novels of P. D. James, who seems to want to take up the Sayers mantle (could it not just be left where it was?), and to write intelligent, middle-brow, slightly verbose novels. But nobody now is likely to doubt the durability of P. D. James, or to deny that she satisfies a need in crime readers for greater depth of characterization, more sensitive understanding of motive, more intelligent portrayal of contemporary milieus.

The crime novel is joyously plural. All types will go on

being written, and will fluctuate in and out of fashion. Most people will enjoy many kinds: nobody would imagine from what I have written here that among my favorite writers of the last two or three decades are Ross Macdonald and Ruth Rendell, or that my hot tip for the future would be Sheila Radley. If I were advising a beginning writer, I would not say go in this or that direction, adopt this or that style. There is room for all types of crime book, and who would be so foolhardy as to predict fashion? I would keep the advice severely practical: carry a notebook with you everywhere; learn about semicolons; leave a few spelling mistakes in your manuscript to make your editor feel good.

But I expect in the end my hobbyhorses would creep in, and I would tell him to remember that as a crime writer he is "not Prince Hamlet, nor was meant to be," and that he'd much better pitch his ambitions to being an attendant lord, or, indeed, "almost, at times, the Fool." And, pedagogue to the last, I might be unable to refrain from adding Mr. Sleary's advice in *Hard Times*: "People mutht be amuthed."

The Mirrored Badge

Rex Burns

Police work takes place on the rough edge of social conflict, and so—for me—the police procedural is almost by definition a novel of manners. Granted, the range of those manners may be narrow or foreign to the reader, and the people possessing them may seem to very ill-mannered indeed; but the criminal society is nonetheless a society, and the policeman's life is inextricably mingled with it. The fictional detective, then, becomes an agent by which to explore this darker side of our American experience—and perhaps the darker side of our individual psyches, as well.

Entailed in this concept of the police story as a novel whose subject reflects contemporary society is a belief in the value and continuing freshness of realistic writing. Some writers can't contain their stories in an undistorted mirroring of the world around them; and I have been captured by and deeply envy the spiraling, dizzying creations of the free-ranging imagination found in such novelists as García Márquez and Roger Zelazny. But the police story is earthbound and time bound, and the intensity I seek to create is the intensity of the crystalline now: the clarity, the sharpness, the palpability of a present world on the page that becomes real by winning its existence through mirroring and rivaling the world we experience.

This is not journalism. A police story is not a police report. Realistic or otherwise, the novel, unlike life, has its own structure which in some way establishes a beginning, middle, and end. This means that the world of fiction is far more coherent, far more ordered and meaningful, than the world in which we live. This fictional structure makes its demands on characterization, event, setting—in short, on all the elements that make up this thing called the novel. One might think, for example, of the fictional character as always being on-stage—that his every thought and action delivers to the audience some contribution to the book's conclusion, whether that conclusion is on the level of event or meaning. Those aspects of life which do not contribute happen offstage. In real life, of course, there is no on- or offstage; we go in a dozen different ways at once, and the only curtain is death. Not so in the kind of fiction where something has to happen and where the audience expects a rising curve of tension. And whereas journalism is interested only in those momentary facets of a person's life that catch the light of headlines, fiction strives to find a deeper architecture in a character's existence—a sequence of related causes and actions that culminates in the final climactic event and which also, in some way, rounds off the series in some kind of all-embracing meaning. The result for the mystery writer is the paradox of an art form that, while working within its own strict formal requirements, attempts to recreate the effect and appearance of contemporary life with its everyday formlessness.

This paradox is not new to novel writing, but it is of vital importance to detective stories. Much crime is chaotic, an eruption into the ordered, public surface of our lives from some dark reservoir below—an intrusion, that is, of life's formlessness. Different times have different names for this darkness: Kaos, Satan, the Id. Regardless of its label now or in the future, it exists, and the detective writer is faced with the problem of trying to explore the irrational in some rational manner. In much detective fiction, the explanation is simplistic and the revelation of this motive leads to the solution of the crime: greed, envy, hatred. In the best fictions, these motives are seen as agents of something more profound—a gnawing spiritual starvation, perhaps, as in Dostoevski, or a self-contempt that negates any sense of humanity, as in Graham Greene. For some, the explanation is less abstract—social dislocations or economic systems; for others, the cause lies in the realm of cosmic irony. Regardless of the explanation, the question the writer asks is "Why?" Why this hatred? Why this greed? Whereas the detective wants only to solve the crime, the writer is faced with the need to explain it. And of course he does not always find explanations. Perhaps the chaos will always outdistance the reasoning human mind that tries to encompass it. But the attempt is made, and that attempt can lead the mystery writer to the limits of explaining the possibly inexplicable.

One such limitation is that the "complete fiction"—the all-embracing novel—will never be written. And that includes *Finnegans Wake*. Life is too protean, too vast, too charged with energy ever to be captured. Only larger or smaller elements of it can be reflected with more or less intensity. Consequently, for me, realism is the mode that offers the best chance to carve out a segment of contemporary life and to make it coherent—to reconstruct it into an admittedly artificial but convincingly mimetic portrait of the world I live in.

Why crime fiction rather than any other kind? Well, I do write other types of fiction, but I haven't been lucky enough to publish them—perhaps because I haven't yet defined clearly enough what it is I'm trying to say in the other modes. But there are less abstract reasons why I turned to detective fiction, and especially to the police procedural. One of the most basic was disgust with the clichés of the genre. The roots of that disgust were in the false portrayals of cops and robbers which, especially in the mass media, can be perilous to viewers who accept them as real. These clichés are most evident on television, as we all know, where a story's true purpose is to attract an audience for the commercials. But the vidiot-types invade the rest of the world, too, including the realm of fiction; and the result there is an increasing emphasis on mindless action and on highly visual scenes that are readily translated into camera angles. There's a palpable decline of insight into character and cause. I wanted to create a police novel that would be, as exclusively as possible, a written form. A novel's not an essay or a film or a biography; it's not philosophy or history. It's something else, and it's this something else that I was after. In the first Gabe Wager novel, written under the sting of this disgust, not one shot is fired. The hero spends most of his time sitting in a car on sur-veillance, and that car never crashes. One reader said, and I still treasure it, "I was really caught up by *The Alvarez Jour-nal*, but I finished it and—now don't take this wrong—I realized that nothing happens. I read it twice and liked it both times, but nothing happens!" Character, setting, atmos-phere; the legal problem of introducing evidence in court; and especially the word, the voice of the narrative: that's what happens in the book. And that's why, I'm convinced, it can never be translated to film—because it's purely a novel and nothing else.

Perhaps that wish was an influence of postmodern fiction; I had not read that much about postmodernist literary theory at the time, but such ideas float around, so maybe, like the flu, I caught it. But unlike the "fabulists," my goal was to achieve a recreation of contemporary reality rather than to launch out into the vertiginous questions of epistemology or phenomenology. I was after—and still seek—the concreteness of our mutually experienced world, and, through that, to glimpse the resonant, subjective world beneath that concreteness. It's this other, darker, private realm that makes everyone's reality different, even though we are all seated at the same table.

A second reason why I turned to police stories from the more "mainstream" (whatever that means) forms is the important role of police work in American society. The Miranda case and a dozen others like it profoundly changed police operations and even philosophies at the time I began writing longer fiction. The cop on the beat became as concerned with legal procedures as with preventing or solving crimes, and sometimes more so. During my tour in the Marine Corps, I served as a regimental legal officer (this at a time when the only requirement for the job was literacy and, preferably, not too much of that). The experience gave me an appreciation for the vast difference between law and justice, an appreciation sharpened later by the interminable series of headlines and news items tracing police frustrations over the rulings of the Supreme Court. I figured that what interested me might be of interest to readers, and I had already learned that it's impossible for me to write anything decent about something I'm not interested in. Thus, the principal challenge of my first two novels is not who did it, but how to prove it in court. In fact, *The Alvarez Journal* and *The Farnsworth Score* name the bad guys in the titles, which is about as up-front as one can be, and the first one ends with the guilty party being caught but the crime continuing, while the second ends with the guiltier party escaping because of a lack in the chain of evidence.

Okay, so a cop story. But why this particular cop? Why a half-breed with the improbable name of Gabe Wager? His core is found in a poem I heard while stationed on Okinawa. It's called "The Gunnery Sergeant," and if I knew who wrote it, I'd give him credit:

There's them that is
and there's them that ain't.
and them that ain't
ain't.

Wager, an ex-Marine who is at home in neither the Chicano world nor the Anglo one, has had to define himself. He did this by establishing and living up to a strict code of dedication and quality that excludes a lot of people. I didn't know at the time that I was reincarnating an archetype, that of the Lone Avenger that peoples so much of American detective fiction. There were simply some very practical benefits to having the man be, in Melville's words, an *isolato*. He could function solely and cleanly on the criminal case without having to worry about the kids' teeth or the dog's vet bill or whether or not the wife can afford that new dish pattern. In other words, the routines of life could be kept offstage to a greater degree and the crime story could be crafted more cleanly and directly than otherwise. As to his name, I wanted to indicate someone who was on the side of the angels and who wasn't afraid to gamble. I also needed a name that would combine the Latin and the English—and be a bit unusual. The result: Gabriel Villanueva Wager.

Wager's hard struggle for self-definition in a world that has its labels all ready to apply has given him a rigidity that is both strength and weakness. It is his pride that holds him to the strict code of duty and courage that was innate in him and nurtured by his eight years in the Marine Corps (he enlisted at age sixteen). Likewise, it is his pride that makes it difficult for him to forgive himself or others for mistakes. I saw this as a kind of tragic flaw, an inflexibility that—given the situation—could be either good or bad. In *Alvarez* we see the good side of it; he won't cut corners despite temptations, and the result is a solid case that holds up in court. In perhaps my favorite of the series, *Angle of Attack*, his per-

sonal code works against him and forces him outside the legal
restrictions to answer to a higher law, one not written in
society's books but on every man's heart. Unfortunately this
rigidity turned out to be a strategic error on my part: it
ossified his ability to change and grow through the series.
This problem is compounded by Wager's lack of humor. I
gave him absolutely no sense of humor. To me, that's funny—
the guy is surrounded by the comedy as well as the sadness
of life, but is too stiff to laugh. To me, it's a classic Bergsonian
situation: the actor holds rigidly to his course no matter how
the environment might change. But I've subsequently discovered that my own sense of humor is a tad aberrational,
and not many readers laugh when I do. Now I'm stuck with
him, and I sometimes wonder who really does have the last
laugh.

Of course he will change—we all do. However, that change
will have to be gradual in order to be convincing, because I
see each individual novel as a single chapter in a larger work
that has its own architecture of fifteen volumes. Why I settled
on fifteen, I don't know; perhaps it was only that the first
novel had fifteen chapters. But the point is that the entire
structure should have consistency, so any change between
novels will have to be carefully prepared for and thoroughly
believable. Whether or not I reach the last volume depends
on a lot of things, not the least of which is luck, and there's
no sense speculating about that now.

One of the pressures toward change in Wager is reader
response. A number of correspondents apparently like the
man better than I do, and they want to know more about his
personal life, to see him loosen up a little bit, maybe even to
drink a beer with him. I seriously doubt if he'll change that
much, because he is a tough man in a tough life; it's too easy
to begin to relax, and then one's grip loosens. A second
pressure is something I had not anticipated: the need for
novelty. Fortunately for us as citizens, crime falls into types

and patterns that, after a while, become familiar and even predictable to the detective. But what's beneficial in real life is death to the novelist. In an effort to explore the less familiar, Wager was early on transferred from the Organized Crime Unit, which dealt mostly with narcotics cases, to Homicide. Then he was given a partner, Max-the-Axe Axton, as a foil (and a sense of humor). Then the geographical range of his responsibilities was broadened to include the rest of Colorado rather than just the city of Denver. In one of his latest adventures, he takes a vacation. But throughout all these changes in the environment around him, I'm trying to keep his character not static but consistent. One result of placing him in different situations is that it enables me to look closely at different occupations and various strata in local society. *Strip Search*, for example, explores the stripper and porno world in east Denver; *Avenging Angel* deals with the excommunicated Mormon community that was shooting up the West a few years ago. Rodeo is the setting for the current adventure. In this search for novelty, I don't know how the next yarn will be structured or where it will be placed; but that, of course, is part of the challenge and the joy of this racket—there's a freedom to fail or to succeed, but above all, there's a freedom.

Perhaps my way of writing reinforces a sensitivity to the need for consistent change in the series. I like to alternate writing Gabe Wager novels with other types of fiction. These range from sprawling historical yarns to sports stories, and only a couple of them are any good. But it's an exercise of different muscles and a search for different directions away from the tightly constricting confines of detective fiction. So far, the only practical benefit is that when I come back to the Wager series, it's with the perspective of a different kind of writing and with the relief of greeting old friends and enemies on familiar ground. And, like all of us who return home after a long time, I see things I didn't see before.

As to the actual sitting down at the typewriter, I try to write five or six days a week for at least three or four hours, preferably in the morning. Fortunately my teaching schedule allows me the afternoon and evening classes that are so popular at a downtown university, and I can generally keep to this schedule. It takes about a year for a Gabe Wager to go from the first sentence to the final proof of copy, but only about six months of that is actually spent on creating the work. When a book's finished, I'll take a couple days off; but then inner pressures start building up again and I don't feel comfortable unless I'm writing on another story of some kind.

Currently I'm working on a film script based on a not-so-good novel I wrote several years ago. I'm doing it for a number of reasons, not the least of which is that I hope to sell it—for the "mid-range" writer, there's more money in films than there is in books. But I also want to try my hand at another form, and in so doing to reclarify for myself the essential differences between film and fiction. Interestingly, the cutting and paring, the totally visual emphasis which filmscripts require, have enabled me to see weaknesses in the novel that I had not clearly perceived before. It has also drained the story of a tremendous amount of nuance and complexity, things which a director and cameraman will have to recreate in their own way if they want it. And it's convinced me that even if this script is a success, I am first of all a writer of novels.

Whether or not I was born to write is an unanswerable question. I don't remember a time when I did not enjoy books, and in fact I used to be pushed outside to play because it wasn't considered natural for a boy to spend a sunny afternoon with his nose in a book. I do know that my dad wanted to be a writer; his dream was to retire from the Navy, edit a weekly country newspaper, and write fiction. He didn't get his chance, so maybe that was a spur to my own dreams. But the fact is, I was writing stories before he was killed in World War II and cannot recall a time when I wanted to do anything else. Maybe the urge to write is genetic, but let's leave those speculations to the probers and prodders and stop fussing over protozoic impulses.

The most vital if not always the most reliable critic a writer has is himself. But anyone who publishes submits his work to assessment by the world, and if he's lucky the world will respond. This comes in the form of friends, or ex-friends who think they see themselves in a novel, or—the best kind of response—letters from readers who have been moved enough to write you. I particularly enjoy and take pride in those painfully written ones that come from prisons and reformatories. But the majority of responses are from people who get paid to assess your work, critics and reviewers. Critics are far more important to the reader than to the writer. Fortunately, the ill or good they do an author is less than they assume, but people do read book reviews, and in the highly competitive business of marketing fiction, notice of any kind is far, far better than no notice at all. The effect of critics on writers varies, certainly, with the critic and with the writer. I read my clippings, though in the field of detective fiction they generally tend to be reviews and summaries of the story rather than considered assessments. This latter kind of criticism is rare for genre writers, and when one does come along I pay particular attention to it out of respect for the person who took the time and effort to think about what I wrote. Sometimes this respect is merited, sometimes it isn't. But even a faulty review or criticism can offer insight to one's own work. That is, a critic, like an editor, often lights on something in the novel that bothers him— something that doesn't seem to click. He then goes on to explain why it doesn't work, but that's not so important—let the critic show the reader that he himself could be a better detective story writer if he really wanted to, that's fine. What's important to me is that a reader has had a problem, and it's my job to determine first if the problem was my fault or the critic's; and, if mine, how I might handle the issue better in the future. If I achieved what I set out to achieve, let it stand; if not, then the solution is mine to discover, and mine alone. I've learned that no one—agent, editor, critic—can write for you. The burden and the prize are your own.

There's another kind of criticism, also rare for genre writers but growing more widespread with the rise of academic study of the fields. I suppose it comes under the heading of literary history, and its purpose is less to review a particular work at the time of publication than to judge a writer's entire collection of work and to place it in relation to other writers in the field. I approach this kind of criticism very, very gingerly, very defensively; it is often written by critics who consider themselves to be judges and even executioners, and among whom balance and sanity and generosity can be nasty words. Even the few good ones—and thank God there are some—are to be read with great care. A writer's ego is his most vulnerable point, and the ease with which it can be wounded or seduced is appalling. Add to that the loneliness of the long-distance writer, and a few words from a major literary critic can badly skew the unwary author's vision of himself and his world. I do not know of any writer who was ever helped in his craft by a critical review and of only a very few who were helped in any major way by editors. Fortunately, this kind of critical attention is usually reserved for "mainstream" writers, and the rest of us are free to follow Joyce's dictum for the survival of authors: Secrecy, Silence, Cunning.

But the formal study of detective fiction and crime writing has increased, though it is by no means a new phenomenon. Popular Culture studies have been around in universities at least since the 1950s, and when one considers that American literature itself wasn't a respected academic pursuit until just before World War II, that's a fairly long time. Generally, these approaches are less literary and more cultural. That is, instead of evaluating the novel on the grounds of any intrinsic literary merit (the usual assumption is that it does not have any), the work is studied as a document which indicates trends in popular tastes or mass values or the zeitgeist of an age. This is fine: it gives the writer some needed exposure, provides jobs for academics, and doesn't really hurt anyone. It may even lure students into the world of fiction and away from the television set, and I truly believe that the exercise of rational speculation about books of any kind may be almost as beneficial to humanity as constructing a new killer gas or orchestrating another corporate raiding party.

Still, for the author who is sensitive to this kind of attention—and I never met one who wasn't—such assessments are as dangerous as those mentioned above and for the same reasons. But what this kind of comparison and "placing" can do, and this much is healthy, is lead the writer to measure himself against others who have gone before. Forget comparing one's self to contemporary writers, though it's nice to win an Edgar for best this or that. The real comparison is to those who have been established by time: Poe, Doyle, Hammett, Chandler, Christie, Simenon, etc. And the benefit of the comparison is that the writer begins to study how these people achieved their effects. In my own case, I had read very little in the mystery genre before I wrote *Alvarez*. I'm still often embarrassed by questions from mystery buffs who know far more about the field's history and practitioners than I do. Out of self-defense, I had to begin reading; and to save time, I began reading the best known. My affinity for Hemingway led me to Simenon, and from him I learned a greater appreciation for the nuance of setting—the single note of color or mood that registers on the mind of the almost passive detective and, without being a clue exactly, contributes to an understanding of motive. I liked, too, the speed with which Simenon's stories develop, and the way the dialogue often implies more than it states. And I compared myself to Simenon's achievements but in a way different from the usual competitive stance. Rather, the comparison was by way of analogy: Simenon got this certain effect in this certain way, how could I get an analogous effect without copying his method? Gradually, the terseness of description in my stories has eased, especially when dealing with a Western landscape whose vastness demands hyperbole instead of compression. But its use for adding meaning to the narrative or under- standing of the protagonist hasn't changed. For me, as for Simenon, description provides setting, a choral commentary on the action, and a means whereby the protagonist can be explored obliquely. As for placing myself historically or de- velopmentally in relation to Simenon or any other writer, I'll leave that up to the one critic who is most often right—time.

I learn from my contemporaries, too. Robert Parker makes a nice use of one-liners and wisecracks that is, I believe, an American art form. Certainly it's in the long tradition of hard-boiled detective story writing, and with it Parker cap- tures the grittiness and wit of street life. In the use of lan- guage, Elmore Leonard demonstrates what can be done when the patterns of the spoken word are captured on the page. This is part of another tradition in American literature, that of raising to artistic levels the everyday speech of curb and shop. One might argue that Franklin did it, and Emerson; certainly Whitman sang his barbaric yawp, and Kerouac as well as the Beat poets worked in the jazz rhythms of urban slang. Detective fiction has done its large share in broad- ening the concept of "proper" literary language, and Leonard is adept at bringing the tradition into the 1980s. Tony Hill- erman has singled out a fascinating corner of America, the Navajo culture, and achieves a very difficult balance between telling a fast-moving story and giving us a glimpse into the core of an alien way of life. Evan Hunter's skill with plotting and with juggling a variety of story lines is both daring and instructive, and I've learned a lot from studying his work. John D. MacDonald demonstrates that a detective story can have room for reflection and commentary without losing its momentum, provided the writer has MacDonald's skill; and Lawrence Sanders shows how a mystery yarn can be used to probe the moral questions rising from today's issues. The roll call could go on because the range and quality of writing in the field is impressive, but the point should be made by now that writing, and maybe detective story writing in particular, is continually evolving under the impetus of shared ideas and techniques. Writers do look at each other's productions—they're almost forced to whether they want to or not—and as any craftsman knows, if you see something that works, you borrow it and adapt it for your own.

Where might all this development be headed? I don't know. I understand there are some critics who assert that the criticism is more important than the text being criticized, and that these critics will be the ones to give future direction to the evolution of fiction. Not very damned likely. That kind of criticism branches off into its own realm of creativity, using the text as a springboard of inspiration and an excuse for a kind of narcissistic performance. The truth is that the writer leads and the critic follows. And since writers aren't sure of the road they travel until they put their foot on it, predictions about writing's future are tenuous at best. But I think the demands will be consistent: the strong demand for exciting stories that baffle and frighten and entertain, the lesser demands for stories that give as much pleasure in the play with language as they do in the play with action, for tales that provide insight into the conflict between right and wrong, for yarns that seem to capture the way we live now. I suspect, too, that the line between "genre" and "mainstream" fiction, which has become quite thin already, will continue to fade as the quality of writing continues to increase. Already, the classification of novels into mysteries and nonmysteries seems to be less a descriptive term and more a marketing device. There will always be a nucleus of whodunits around which the genre clusters. But witness the struggle to define the term "mystery novel" and to have a definition that will fit the variety of books accepted as mysteries. And there are those books not labeled mysteries that have all the characteristics, such as John Hawkes's fine tale, *The Lime Twig*.

I think, too, we will see the continuation of the hard-boiled detective story and the police procedural; both of these seem imbedded in the American literary fabric. The cozier English-style mystery featuring a puzzle and a literate, amateur sleuth will be with us, too, it's safe to say. But what new forms, mutating out of a wedding with science fiction or historical romance or other neighboring genres, will evolve is anyone's guess and part of the excitement of watching the field. Whatever directions do evolve, I'm certain they will be based on the problems and conflicts of contemporary life, and their underlying aim will be to explore and provide new configurations for defining and resolving those conflicts.

One salient area of conflict is the political, and by definition it always will be. But it's surprising how few mysteries have been based primarily on political topics. We have a number of other kinds of stories that portray political life and themes, beginning, in the recent past, with Henry Adams's *Democracy* and coming down to *The Last Hurrah* and beyond. Yet even with such writers as Margaret Truman, politics seems to serve the mystery writer more as background or setting rather than subject or motive. Political issues do surface as causes for murder and mayhem in adventure yarns focusing on terrorism and espionage. But those tales don't always fit comfortably among mysteries, because they often lack the element of detection. Perhaps the political issue hasn't moved firmly into the subject matter of detective fiction because the American political system is more open to dissent than the systems of many other nations. Also, we seem to have very few times in our history when such issues have been worth killing for, or when writers have been viewed as embodying our political consciences. That, of course, may change, and if it does, I think the detective story will change with it. But so far, our national violence has tended to be apolitical and dedicated to more concrete goals than ideology.

I don't think the reason has been the oft-bruited one that mystery stories are inherently conservative and therefore shy away from raising questions that might challenge the political structure. As I understand this argument, it's that mystery tales, since they are concerned with reestablishing order after a (usually) homicidal disorder, have a bias toward the status quo. The police, being servants of the state, support the ruling class; and the criminal, being a threat to that class, must be captured so society's safety can be assured. But what if the ruling class is the proletariat? Does this make the Communist mystery writer a conservative? If so, do the terms "conservative" and "liberal" have any fixed meaning as critical tools? I think a distinction should be made between crimes of a political nature and those of human nature, and I think, further, that most American mysteries tend to deal with the latter. It's not unheard of for detective writers or their heroes to speak loudly against the state; Dashiell Hammett was, after all, fingered by the House un-American Activities Committee and made no bones about his Communist leanings. And we don't have to look too deeply into the stories of Raymond Chandler to see that the villains are hardly distinguishable from such aggressive capitalists as William Randolph Hearst or others who, in Chandler's eyes, betrayed democratic ideals and decencies for greed and power. Yet the novels of both these writers end with order restored; the victim is somehow recompensed, and the villain is punished. Obviously, there's more going on than a simplistic political analysis of the genre would allow, and one is tempted to believe that the theory doesn't comfortably fit the data.

Indeed, if writers' sympathies seem to lie in any general direction, it's with the underdog—the victims of society—and even at times with those who victimize others in a desperate attempt to keep from sinking under the weight of an unfair social system. My own feeling is that more mystery writers identify with the outright rebel than with the social conservative, and even Robert Parker's virulent law-and-order pronouncements call less for the punishment of violators of political law and more for the violators of moral law.

The fact is that mystery yarns have to be solved. Social order may be restored as a side effect of that given, but often the "larger picture" isn't even considered—or it contributes a wry, bitter effect to the story's conclusion. I think the proper frame of reference for viewing the restoration of order is not a political spectrum but an artistic pattern. The novel is an artistic structure with a beginning, a middle, and an end; and it's possible that the mystery story which ends with a restoration of harmony may be seen as a species of comedy.

Without getting embroiled in the centuries-old debate over what distinguishes tragedy from comedy, let's simply use one widely accepted modern definition of the terms: tragedy ends sadly, comedy ends happily. In addition, tragedy usually involves characters of some importance to a society, though—as with Willy Loman—that importance may be symbolic rather than financial or political. This, of course, opens the door for major characters to enter the realm of comedy, and so the genres become even more confused. But I think the argument is fairly clear—by reestablishing a harmony of some kind, the detective story is, in effect, doing what the comedy does after the disruptions of the plot. Does that make comedy a politically conservative form? Or a liberal one? Surely those who argue that the very form of the detective story makes it automatically conservative should also argue that

Shaw in *Major Barbara* or *Man and Superman* was writing a drama dedicated to preserving the status quo because of the reestablishment of harmony at the conclusion of these plays. Unless the novel or play has a political message, then, the question of whether or not the form itself is conservative seems to be irrelevant.

If the form can in any generic way be labeled conservative, it must be in a much broader sense that transcends political dichotomies and enters the realm of morality. Sometimes brashly, sometimes hesitantly, detective stories assert the superiority of such things as honesty, goodness, humanness, courage, over such things as lying, evil, cruelty, cowardice. In this way, the detective story tries to conserve universal human values, an effort that most political groups soon find to be embarrassing and impractical. Moreover, detective fiction asserts what is, to my understanding of the world, a pretty radical idea: that the crime should be solved and the evildoers punished. Try going to Washington, D.C.—or your own state capital—and spreading that idea about; you'll be labeled a subversive by politicians and businessmen of all political inclinations. It seems to me that the American fictional detective tends to eschew politics for a personal moral stance that supports human values that have not and will not change. Let Gabe Wager speak for himself on that, from the conclusion of *The Farnsworth Score*: "There were cops with pride—men with pride—who tried not to play games with their lives or anyone else's."

Writing about Balzic

K. C. Constantine

I started writing crime fiction because I'd had no success selling anything else I'd written. I'd sent some short stories to an agent who'd been recommended by a friend, but the agent said she wouldn't even try to sell the stories because the market for them was either terrible or nonexistent, I forget which word she used. It was just as well, because the stories were lame, though at the time, of course, I thought they were terrific stuff, subtly structured and deeply symbolical, etc. The agent told my friend to ask me if I had any mysteries. "They always sell," she said. I was revulsed. Naturally.

Shortly thereafter, I went to a newsstand to buy a paper, the Sunday *New York Times*, no doubt, because at that time the local papers were beneath my pretensions; and, with my agent's advice rattling reluctantly in my mind, I observed carefully the many paperbacks by Carter Brown, Ross Macdonald, John MacDonald, Mickey Spillane, Agatha Christie, Georges Simenon, et al., in the wire racks near the cash register. I say I observed them carefully, because I had carefully not observed them since I'd last bought one of Spillane's books when I was a senior in high school. When the line moved up and my turn came, I asked the clerk if he sold many of those mysteries. "Can't keep 'em in stock," he said.

I bought the paper, went to my car, and drove off in the direction of the ruins of the train station. Before I'd gone two blocks I had schemed the barest plot of *The Rocksburg Railroad Murders*, though that title didn't come till much later. I don't remember much about writing that book except being driven by the notion that I had to write something that somebody was going to buy. I'd been writing for many years and hadn't sold a sentence and those two facts had just about chewed up what was left of my pretensions. I decided that if what I wrote wasn't good enough to move a publisher to spend the money and effort to print it, then it was time to quit kidding myself; I had been bitching about all the hacks whose books were on the best-seller lists long enough. So I wrote it, blundering through the problem I'd had with every other novel I'd written or tried to write, i.e., I didn't know how to make a plot. And if you're going to write a mystery, or a detective story, or crime fiction, or whatever anybody calls it, you had better know how to make a plot. It's one thing to read what E. M. Forster said about "the king dying and the queen dying of grief" and "the king dying" being a story and "the king dying and the queen dying of grief" being a plot, but it's something else to do. Maybe Forster knew what he was talking about, and maybe I could sit around and discuss the hell out of those notions after I'd had a couple of beers, but when it came time to put my fingers on the typewriter, I didn't know how to do it. And while you might be able to dance around a plot in a so-called straight novel, i.e., you might try playing with time and tense and resolution and all those other abstractions people use when they talk about fiction, if you said you were going to write a novel about a crime and how it was solved, well, you can only shadowbox so long: sooner or later, you have to say how the king died and why the queen died of grief.

After I finished that book and sent it off to the agent, I started right in on another, and when I finished that one and sent it to her, I started a third, all with the same central characters set in the same locale. Publishers' rejections continued to arrive, but for some reason they didn't have the same impact. Somehow, I'd sensed that I was on to that elusive thing called plot. Before I'd finished the third, my agent called and told me that Saturday Review Press had bought the first two. I was an amateur no longer.

Writing those three books taught me some hard truths: a story is a story and writing is writing no matter what the subject, and calling one kind of story and writing "serious" and another kind "formula writing" is a dissociation made only by snobs or ignorant people. Since I was both ignorant and a snob before I tried to write them, I had to dump a load of dubious education in order to be able to write them. Nothing will do that as quickly as picking up a pen and staring at blank paper, *knowing* that anybody can write a mystery. Looking back at it now, I'm puzzled about why I thought that writing a mystery should be called "formula writing." I'd never heard anyone accuse Shakespeare of "formula writing" when he wrote all those sonnets, and a sonnet has about as rigid a formula as can be imagined. But there was something about writing "mysteries" that smacked of a cop-out, especially when I knew that all I had to do was fill blank paper with easy words in simple sentences in a direct route from the discovery of a body to the arrest of the murderer. Nothing to it. Any one can do it....

My father was an immigrant, as were my mother's parents. My father attended the equivalent of American elementary school in Russia, but he never went to school in this country until after he was married, and then it was to attend an art school in New York City. He lasted only until his money ran out. My mother was allowed to finish the third grade before her father sent her to work in a mill. My parents, like many others of their generation and circumstances, were almost obsessively concerned that their children should at the very least finish high school, which my brother and I did. I went on to a private liberal arts college run in association with the Presbyterian church, though my recollection of how that college was chosen or why I was the one to go to college and my brother, who is older, was not, are among many events in my life I've never fully understood.

My mother taught me to read before I started the first grade, and somehow she managed to find the money to buy books for me all through my childhood. When I was in college she gave more than a hundred books to the library of the elementary school I'd attended. Now and then she allowed me to buy comic books, provided they were the non-violent kind, which I took to school and traded to get the kind I wasn't supposed to read. What stands out in my mind is that I hear a lot of dialogue in movies or on TV that reminds me of the dialogue that appeared in those comic books my mother thought were not good for me.

While my mother and the public schools were trying to refine my reading, my father was training me in an altogether different way. He was both a craftsman and an artist and did everything from restoring antiques, both real and forged, to repairing damaged statuary for the local Catholic churches. Before the Depression, he made a lot of money painting billboards, but he also painted for very little money those signs that used to be in the windows in every butcher shop and grocery. He painted walls and houses and portraits of people's pets. He also painted landscapes, still lifes, portraits, and whole churches, floor to cupola, and when he wasn't doing anything else he was painting flowers on the lids of five-gallon paint cans and turning them into trays. He did a lot of crap for money (he painted four "portraits" of the same dog, for example), but everything he did was decent and some of his paintings are extraordinary. He exhibited his work all over the Northeast and had at least three one-man shows, but he was the least vocal man I've ever known and so he never made much money at it.

The thing I remember most about him is that he never went anywhere without pencils and a small pad. He was always sketching faces while we were on a streetcar or bus and he could do it without seeming to. He'd hold the pad down in his lap and stare off, then he'd look down and make a few quick marks, and within seconds, it seemed to me, he'd have made a remarkable likeness of someone who wasn't even aware he or she was being observed. Without ever talking about it, my father showed me that the subject for art was where you found it, though it was many years before I even began to think about it in those terms.

In elementary school, I displayed a little talent for drawing, and I was chosen to attend art classes run by the City of Pittsburgh in Carnegie Museum, and, except for the summers, I went every Saturday morning for three years until I was about fourteen. I had to take a bus and then a streetcar and it was a long ride to the Museum, so I naturally mimicked my father's habit of studying faces. I couldn't bring myself to sketch them the way he did; I suppose I was too embarrassed. But I'd try to sketch them from memory when I got home. The art classes themselves frustrated the hell out of me because the emphasis seemed to be on releasing creativity rather than on teaching technique and also because we were made to paint in tempera on a very grainy, grayish paper. I learned very soon that I wasn't meant to paint anything in tempera, especially on that paper. It's funny that the thing I remember most about those classes is that damned paper. I couldn't do anything on it.

One day my father found me trying to draw a face I'd seen on the streetcar. All I remember about the conversation that followed is that he explained to me in great detail how a face is divided and how you measure its parts against its other parts in order to draw it, e.g., a nose is as long as the ears in a hypothetically normal face and the mouth is as wide as the distance between the pupils of the eyes, and once you knew these hypothetical distances it was fairly easy to spot the variations that appear in every real face. I could, of course, have gotten more or less the same instruction from any basic drawing book, but it made a permanent impression coming from my father, even though it didn't make me an artist by any means.

When I was very young, five at the oldest, some policemen came into our neighborhood and began to question people about something. If I knew what they were talking about then, I certainly don't remember it now; what struck me was that when the cops approached some people I knew, they suddenly couldn't speak English, or American as my father always called it. Now I knew that those people spoke American, because I heard them talking every day, yet there they were, seemingly unable to speak anything but the language they had learned as children. The immediate lesson was that cops were not to be trusted; years passed before I understood the depth of mistrust the people in that neighborhood had for anyone remotely resembling an agent of the government.

What I'm getting at is that, very early on, I observed something that caused me to pay close attention to the way people speak and do not speak, to what they say and how they say it, and to what they do not say and how they go about avoiding having to say it. We all learn this, of course, but for some reason, that incident left me with a pronounced inclination to study the way people talk, their rhythm, their pauses, inflections, evasions, etc.—so much so that I seemed not to have learned to talk myself, or at least not well enough to feel comfortable with people I'd just met. (It's only in the last few years that I've begun to pay as much attention to my own speech to hear what I'm saying or not saying and how it affects other people and why. I'm still much better at listening to others than I am at listening to myself.) I believe I can recognize a person's speech as easily as I can recognize his face. Notice that I said "believe." I'm not setting myself up as an expert about this; all I'm saying is that watching my father sketch faces (and later being told how he did it) and seeing reasonably intelligent people when being questioned by cops suddenly forget how to speak a language they knew very well have both greatly influenced how I write and what I write about.

I don't, for example, spend a lot of time trying to describe people, other than to note something about them physically that may have influenced the way they behave. Somebody said—I think it was Somerset Maugham—that the world is not the same place for a short man as it is for a tall one. On the other hand, I'm always trying to define characters by letting them speak. I'm always playing with the limits of misspelling and I'm always trying to figure out how to use punctuation to sustain or interrupt the flow of a character's speech, even though I know there is only so much you can do with the alphabet and even though, when I do it to my satisfaction, I know it annoys copy editors and proofreaders, it probably won't mean much to some readers, and it will probably irritate others. I think that a writer who can put three characters in a scene and can write several lines of dialogue without attribution and without confusing the reader has paid attention to his characters and has invested in them qualities that no amount of descriptive, expository prose can convey. One of the things that strikes me about Georges Simenon is that he can write several paragraphs of exposition, write one line of unattributed dialogue, and then go on to more exposition and leave no doubt about which character has been speaking. It looks simple, and it is, but it is not simple to do.

When your parents believe fervently, as mine did, in the necessity of formal education and when one of them abetted the process, you're bound to run into problems, the biggest one being something called Literature. As a result of my mother's early teaching, I was always on the lookout for a story that taught me something and also made me feel good; those were, after all, her goals for teaching me to read. However, when teachers of Literature tried to make me read something that some other teacher of Literature (or potentate of Education) had decided *was* Literature, then I had problems. Everybody remembers reading stuff like that: *The Mill on the Floss* and *The Rise of Silas Lapham* come quickly to mind. Shakespeare didn't do much for me either. *Julius Caesar* was required reading my senior year in high school, and I got into an awful scene with a nice woman teacher who wanted to know why I was screwing up her tests about the play. I beat around the bush for a long time because I didn't want to hurt her feelings, but finally she told me to stop the nonsense and tell her what I didn't like. "I don't like it," I said, "because it's a bunch of crap. It's supposed to be a play and nobody talks like that."

That year I was on a Western kick, and I'd gone through every Zane Grey in the school library and was trading around the paperbacks of Luke Short and Max Brand and reading all the pulp magazines I could scrounge. Nobody I knew talked like the cowboys, Indians, horse soldiers, marshals, and outlaws in those books and stories either, but their dialogue seemed a lot closer to the speech of people I knew than anybody Shakespeare wrote about. (Ridiculous as it seems, I actually thought people in Shakespeare's time talked like that and that all he was doing was writing what he heard. It never occurred to me that he hadn't heard Julius Caesar or any other Roman say anything, but nobody told me otherwise and I was too confused, ignorant, arrogant, and embarrassed to ask.) But my problem was really between me and my parents, only I didn't know it, and I was taking it out on sincere ladies full of good intentions who were trying to sneak some culture into me.

That problem got lots worse when I landed in the college run by Presbyterians. My first two years there were provocative and aimless. I encountered the Bible for the first time, and I also ran into some serious snobs and bigots. Though both my parents were deeply religious and though I attended church regularly with them (even serving as an altar boy for a couple of years), I knew almost nothing about Christianity for these contrary reasons: all church services for the first eighteen years of my life were conducted in Russian; my father, though he had been born in Russia, considered himself American to the point that he refused to teach me Russian and spoke it with my mother only when they wanted to keep me in the dark. Church, then, for me was a series of rituals performed in a foreign language, except for confession and for the instructions I was given to serve the altar.

I know it sounds preposterous, but it's true: I went to church at least three times a month, many more times during Lent, knelt, crossed myself, took communion, lighted candles, dropped nickels into the collection basket, all when I was told to, and all I knew about what it meant was what I learned from the popular myths and without giving any of them more than a moment's thought. I honestly don't know what I thought all that was about. Then I was plunged into classes on the Bible and mandatory chapel services four times a week, all packaged in sturdy Calvinist wrappings, and I also found myself living, along with the usual run of freshmen, among dozens of students who were preparing to become ministers and missionaries.

To befuddle me further, the priest back home decided during my freshman year to start offering the liturgy and giving his sermons in English, so that when I went home for the summer I discovered that the church I'd been going to for all those years was involved in the same stuff as those Presbyterians, right down to the Apostles' Creed. Never mind all the differences that believers are able to argue about to distinguish their flavor of Christianity from all the others; all I could see and hear were the similarities. I've been confused many times in my life, but never as much as I was then.

There were also some other problems I don't want to go into here, problems between my parents and me that seemed to reflect the confusion and misunderstanding I felt about their religious devotion and how they assumed that I not only understood their beliefs but also shared them with equal intensity. There wasn't a whole lot of talking in my family. I don't want to lay all my problems off on my parents; I was doing some dumb things all on my own. To shorten the story, by the time the Presbyterians asked me to depart their campus at the end of my fourth semester among them, I had been on academic probation twice, flunked freshman composition twice (among several failures), and managed in the summer vacations to get myself arrested three times. The first two arrests brought only minor repercussions. The third brought me before a judge who thought that what I needed most in life was a little old-fashioned discipline; ergo, instead of sending me to the county workhouse for a serious number of months, he gave me the choice of enlisting in the Marine Corps, which, my having done so, would cause him to purge my name from the rolls of convicted felons, which I did and which he did.

And that is how I came to find myself, many months later, prowling the stacks of the library on the second floor of a regimental service club at Camp Lejeune, North Carolina. In hindsight, I can say that one of the more intelligent moves I ever made was enrolling in a typing course in high school and staying with it for two years. Not that I was or am much of a typist, but I was good enough to meet Marine Corps standards, and I often wonder what would have happened to me had I not known how to type. The best thing I can say about the Marine Corps is that the U.S. did not see fit to instruct some other country how to live while I was doing my time as a Remington Raider, the Corps' name for clerk-typists. I feel certain, however, that if it had not been for my meager typing skill and if it had not been for the library on the second floor of that slop chute and the beer bar on the first floor, I would have become round-eyed, slobber-lipped, Section-8 certifiably unfit for service.

The Marine Corps in war has been described more than adequately by any number of writers. But the Marine Corps in peace is another thing, and no matter who tries to describe it, it all comes down to one word: chickenshit. "You can't beat the chickenshit," an old salt once told me in drunken candor. "All you can do is beat the boredom before the next bird decides to squat." Chickenshit is spittin', polishin', shinin', troopin', stompin', and typin' up forms created by the Great God of Military Bureaucracy while some wise-ass with more stripes than you have is telling you in his snarliest tone that you haven't spit, polished, trooped, stomped, or typed fast enough or good enough to suit him; and just when you think you *have* done it fast enough and good enough, here he comes to tell you that if you don't move it, your ass is going on report, which means you'll get to explain to somebody with even more stripes why you have failed to understand the necessity or glory of spittin', polishin', shinin', etc. In the peacetime Marine Corps I heard sensible men pray for war.

However, I did learn to spit and polish, if not with the best of them, then certainly well enough to avoid being put on report; consequently, I had plenty of time to contemplate over the beer in the slop chute just what a certain Presbyterian Ph.D. who had flunked me twice in freshman composition had meant when he'd told me that I "did not know how to make an English sentence."

He was what was called in those days "a dapper little dude."

He spoke whole sentences and didn't use contractions and pronounced every syllable and could pause for effect better than anybody I'd ever heard. He wore tweeds and muted plaids and his shoes were always shined and his clothes pressed and he never slouched and he didn't even lean. He also never looked as though he'd just had a haircut. But every time he talked at me, all I heard was how badly I wrote. My last conversation with him—my last attempt at conversation with him—ended when he told me that my problem was quite simple, really. It was that I "did not know how to make an English sentence."

I used to sit in the slop chute and drink beer and think of all the things I could have replied. I battled privately with my parents' awe of educated people and their obsession with the necessity of getting an education, and with my confusion about all the Bible stories I'd been required to read, and with my recognition that Russian Orthodoxy wasn't fundamentally different from the Presbyterian party line, and with my love of reading stories, and with my failure to translate my love of reading into anything approaching academic success, and with my father's halting, imprecise admonition that he didn't want me to learn Russian because I was an American and should speak American, and with that goddamnable condemnation in that even, confident, modulated voice that I "did not know how to make an English sentence." I was drunk a lot.

One night, as I was wandering through the stacks, I picked up *The True Believer* by Eric Hoffer. I must have thought it was a novel or maybe it had been misplaced in the fiction section, I'm not sure which. I am sure that finding it was another of life's happy accidents, because once I'd started to read it I couldn't let it go. It knocked me out, so much so that I read it through twice over the next couple of days. It was clearly the work of a very well-educated man, but the writing wasn't anything like the usual stuff of textbooks. A

52

guy who happened to bunk next to me, and who happened to have lasted longer in college than I had, told me that Hoffer had never gone to school a day in his life. How he knew that I'm not sure, but I didn't doubt him. I am sure that learning that fact about Hoffer made as much of an impression on me as seeing people forget how to speak English, or American, when they were questioned by cops.

Anyway, one thing led to another, and, not knowing what else to do but feeling compelled to do something, I started copying Hoffer in longhand, and an amazing thing happened: the words that had looked so formidable in type turned out to be just plain old regular words when they came out of the end of my pencil. I copied whole pages and looked at them in the book and in my script and came to the conclusion that if a man who had never gone to school could make sentences like that, well, hell, there was no reason why I couldn't. I remember also having the distinct feeling that Hoffer's sentences were definitely American sentences. They sounded American when I read them aloud, and they looked American when I copied them. Now, of course, it's easy enough to say that my feeling was a reaction to the immaculate, impeccable fart who had dismissed my attempts to meet his course requirements, but then the feeling was intense and I'm sure it was genuine.

No matter. It was a beginning because I started to copy everything I read. And then I made up exercises. I'd copy a paragraph from a book and strike out all the nouns and substitute my own and then I'd do it with the verbs, and so on. Then I'd try to write my own sentences, using the same number of words in the same order about a similar subject. Years later I heard somebody call this the "sedulous ape" theory of learning how to write, but at the time I didn't know it was a theory, never mind that it had a name.

Hoffer wrote in one of his other books that sometimes it doesn't matter whether you're running to something or running away from something. That's a bad paraphrase, but the point is no less true. I was using writing as a way of running from the unholy boredom and the incessant chicken-shit of the Marine Corps, from the patronizing arrogance of that comp teacher, toward a beginning proficiency to make American sentences, toward the beginning of the end of my confusion about all the contrary events that had landed me in the Corps in the first place. At the time I was only vaguely aware of all this. Mostly I told myself that if I didn't do something else with my time, I was going to come out of the Corps with nothing but the memory of a lot of beery nights and headachy mornings.

Then my father died, and I was discharged long before my enlistment was up at the "convenience of the government" to support my mother. Much unpleasantness followed. Despite my nobler aspirations, it turned out that what I'd learned best in the Corps was how to consume beer and argue with the world, and it became obvious even to me that if I soon didn't do something with my life I was going to spend it working crummy jobs or in prison. I then discovered that I had three years of schooling available under the terms of the Korean GI Bill, and once my mother got on her feet, I set about trying to get into another college—any college. No deal, they all said. No matter how they phrased it, it all came back that my two years among the Presbyterians had demonstrated convincingly that I was either stupid or lazy, probably both. That left only one place to go—if they'd have me. But guess who had been promoted to academic dean.

One thing the Marine Corps teaches you is how to grovel while standing at attention. I had learned that passably well, but I surpassed everything the Corps had taught me during my interview with the new academic dean, his creases and diction sharper than before, if such was possible. I vowed penitently to be all that was sober, studious, and sanitary. The only promise I didn't make was to spit-shine his shoes once a week. I wasn't above that; it just didn't get that far.

Because I had no talent for the sciences, no inclination for business, and even less of both for the so-called social sciences, and because nothing had diminished my love of reading, I became an English major. Over the next three years (I spent one whole year making up my previous failures) I read some truly absorbing stuff and a couple of shelves' worth of crud. I never rose above mediocrity as a student, but I was still running, this time from a prospect of dismal jobs or worse; and by some shaky combination of doggedness and luck I got to walk around in a cap and gown in front of an audience that included my mother.

Fast forward to the University of Iowa Writers Workshop where I met Robert V. Williams, who taught the only course I could afford to take. In it, students' stories were the text, and Williams's method was to ask basic questions: What happens in the story? What's the story about? What was the writer trying to do? What ought he have tried to do? Thereafter, it was critical karate with Williams doing his best to keep all the feet reasonably close to the floor. I think I was the only body in the class with just a bachelor's degree. Everybody else in the class had at least one master's, some had two, and a few had Ph.D.s. I never imagined that that many people in one room could talk so glibly about how fiction was or wasn't made. I opened my mouth once in two semesters and never got up the nerve to submit anything I'd written to the class. I did, however, submit a bunch of stuff to Williams, which he allowed me to do, and learned some scarifying things about how much I didn't know. Williams said that yes, of course I did know how to make a sentence, and every once in a while I did put together an acceptable paragraph, but overall I didn't have a clue about how to make a box to carry my stories in. I also needed to learn to spell. He also told me something else: of all those seemingly self-assured vocal gymnasts in the class, only two or three actually wrote; the rest apparently attended class to demonstrate how well they could complain about what other people wrote.

Williams and his wife were very kind to me and my wife and our then-brand-new son. They were generous with their knowledge and their home, especially their kitchen. What I liked most about Williams then and still like about him is that even though he makes his living in academia, he has none of its pretensions. He told me repeatedly that the only sensible way to write fiction was to forget Literature and to make the story tell itself; the worst way was to tell the story as though you constantly had your elbow in the reader's ribs, as though to say, "Hey, look at me. I'm writin'!"

All of the foregoing fed my desire to write and created whatever style I have, because in one way or another it all served to reinforce my notion that there are no better reasons for writing a story than there are for reading one: you want to inform and you want to entertain. Alexander Pope said it better a long time ago; I just happen to have learned that it's still true.

Of all the writers I've learned from—and I think I've learned something from many dozens of them—I suppose the most influential, in addition to Hoffer, have been Ernest Hemingway, E. B. White, and James Thurber. It would take much more space than I've been given here to say what their influence has been, but I think it can be summed up by saying that they were all concerned with economy. They never used five words when three would do. I think the same can be said of Simenon, but I don't really know about that because I've read him only in translation. For a long time I tried not to read people who wrote in American because I was too easily tempted to imitate them. Now it doesn't seem to matter; I don't read much fiction anyway.

One of the questions Robin Winks suggested I answer in this piece was this: "What pleases you or angers you about the current academic discovery of crime fiction?"

First off, I didn't know that academia had discovered crime fiction. Without getting into a harangue about whether *Macbeth* or *The Red and The Black* can be called crime fiction, I'm assuming that what Winks meant by crime fiction includes the kind of stuff I write. Well, I knew that Williams taught a course along those lines because he told me he was going to "teach" one of my books. How he did that is beyond me, but I'm sure he found a way. I also learned that Winks taught a similar course. But I haven't been part of academia since the late sixties, and even then I had only a fuzzy view of what was "in" or "out" among the literati. The thing that's always bothered me about academia is that writing, no matter what kind, was treated much more often than not as though it was and is created in a financial vacuum. Before I got to Iowa City I never once heard a teacher of literature or writing say one word about royalties. In the brief time that I taught in college I found the same to be true. It is as though people who write are supposed to do it only after they've taken a vow of poverty—that way, no one who wants any writing done ever has to talk about paying for it.

Which brings me to the question of critics and whether they are or should be taken seriously. Yes, I do read them, every review that's ever been sent to me, but no, I don't take them seriously. First off, if you can't get a publisher to invest the considerable money and energy it takes to publish your work, then it will never reach the reviewers/critics. Secondly, if a lot of people buy your stuff instead of getting it out of the libraries (bless them every one), what the reviewers/critics have to say won't mean a thing. And if the rev/crits love your stuff but people don't buy it, it doesn't mean a thing either. Most revcrits have been exceedingly complimentary about my stuff, but sales have not come anywhere near equaling their praise. But even if it could be demonstrated beyond doubt that revcrits influence sales, would I take them seriously? How could I? By the time they tell me how much they liked or loathed my last book and why, I'm almost finished with the next one; and since I'm trying not to repeat myself, how could anything a revcrit says about what I've done apply to what I've almost finished doing?

Now, having said that I write mostly for money and that I see no correlation between getting good reviews and making a lot of money and that I don't take revcrits seriously, I have to say that if it wasn't for one revcrit I probably wouldn't be writing at all, or at least not for publication. After my first four books more or less evaporated, I said forget this, and I did for about four years. Then Winks called. Seems he'd found one of my books in a secondhand store somewhere. He suggested that I call Bill Goodman, editorial director for David R. Godine. The three of them were planning to bring out a line of mysteries in trade paperback, two books to a volume. So now, thanks mostly to Winks, my first four books are back in print. And thanks to Goodman and Godine, so are the others. But I still don't write books because of what Winks might or might not say about them after they get published. The only people I pay attention to are me, my wife, and Goodman, in that order.

I must also add, however, that one revcrit, in a long, laudatory piece about the first five of my books, pointed out an error that was important to me personally rather than professionally, i.e., seems I'd made a gross mistake in the chronology of Mario Balzic: in one book I had his father dying when he was a child, and in a later book I had the father dying much later. So, no matter how seriously I regard what the revcrit said, the damage was done as far as the series was concerned. On another level, however, the mistake was a revelation to me psychologically, so much so that I wrote to the revcrit expressing my thanks for having pointed it out, which is the only time I've ever responded to anything a revcrit said.

Which brings me to the last question Winks suggested: are any of my books autobiographical? Certainly they are and certainly they are not. If they weren't, I wouldn't have re-counted those pivotal scenes from my life. I told them be-cause they are what led me to writing in the first place. I don't know anybody who reads a lot who isn't a closet writer, at least when he's absolutely sure nobody's watching. It's as inevitable as a child wanting to imitate the sounds he hears coming from the people around him, provided, of course, the child is physically capable of hearing those sounds and of making them. You connect with the world in a certain way and you respond in that way, unless somebody beats it out of you physically or psychologically. Sometimes a beating only goads you on, but you have to have achieved a certain level of confidence before that can happen. There isn't any question that if my mother had not taught me to read and provided me with all those books before I reached adoles-cence, I would have reacted quite differently to that freshman comp teacher than I did. What my mother did demonstrate to me repeatedly was that reading was worth doing, and despite all the lousy books I've read or been required to read, I've never once thought for a second of not reading. Reading is as natural to me as breathing, and trying to imitate what I read was as logical and psychological as imitating my moth-er's sounds when I was a baby.

Also, anyone who has the law enforced upon him tends to become more acutely aware of how law enforcement works as opposed to how people who have not had the law enforced upon them tend to believe law enforcement is supposed to work. From the time I saw people suddenly forget how to speak American when questioned by cops to the time I went through arrests, bookings, arraignments, hearings, and one trial, I was and continue to be fascinated, intrigued, per-plexed, confused, outraged, horrified, and convulsed with laughter by what comes under the heading of law and order. On another level, I am like everyone else, a creature of our time, and our time has manifested some bizarre and hideous examples that also come under that heading. My father received no mail from his family in Russia after 1937. Now they could have perished in a house fire or they could have been swallowed by the earth in a quake or they could have all eaten the same spoiled food, but it makes more sense to conclude that they stopped writing because they met the same end that millions of others met during Stalin the Terrible's version of law and order. One need only think of the names of certain countries, Nazi Germany, China, Cambodia, Laos, Iran, Argentina, Chile, Cuba, Uganda, to name just a few, to be reminded of the perversions possible in the name of the rule of law and order. (Is it necessary to add that some wonderful things have happened and are happening in America in the name of law and order?)

The point is that no writer in the twentieth century needs to apologize for writing fiction about police and crime, for trying to determine who the police are and why and how they do what they do, for trying to determine who criminals are and why and how they do what they do. Historians and political philosophers and journalists write about great sweeps of events and what they mean; a fiction writer, as E. B. White said, writes about Man by writing about *a* man. I've written about individual crimes in a restricted setting because, I suppose, I am only capable of comprehending events on a small scale. I don't know why this is true any more than I know why I have no capacity for understanding mathematics beyond simple arithmetic or why reading music was an impossible chore or why I am baffled by the simplest mechanical things. What I'm trying to say is that if I were capable and inclined I would perhaps write about monsters like Stalin and what they did to their countries and their peoples. But I am not inclined that way and I apparently do not have the capacity to comprehend such monumental behavior, or at least not in anywhere near the same sense that I am capable of comprehending one man beating another to death with a baseball bat over a gambling scheme that went sour. Whether I'm right or not, it strikes me that to oppose your inclinations and abilities is a fundamental mistake.

But that's for now. I have no idea what I'll be able to comprehend five years from now or what I'll be writing about. If I'm alive and able to hold a pen and type, I'll be scribbling something, because nothing excites me as much as taking the fifty-two letters of the alphabet and the ten marks of punctuation (not counting parentheses, brackets, and ellipses) and trying to make sentences into a story—well, almost nothing.

Some of the Truth

Dorothy Salisbury Davis

It was second-book trouble, only I didn't know anything about second-book trouble at the time. *I* was the trouble. My first book with its modest success had been a fluke. Or divine intervention, although I didn't see how that would have happened, my having recently left the Church. I rewrote the first eighty pages of *The Clay Hand* (1950) many times. The material was rich—murder as an aftermath to a mine disaster, a good newspaperman the victim. I knew the territory and I knew the people, but the story would not come to life. I was coaxing a dead child I could not bring myself to bury. Then, rather violently, I said to myself—or it was said to me—to hell with the beginning; get where you want to be. I wrote a scene in a barroom where the miners were wild with fear and anger, where every attempt to dampen their wrath only fueled it. The scene exploded and I knew the book was about to take off. I went outdoors and walked up and down the meadow saying over and over, "I am a writer, I am a writer...." That has to have been my best moment as a writer, and God knows, I have gone back and relived it in the many times I've needed courage since.

I find the joys of writing rare but exquisite. Few things give me such pleasure as striking an image that says in a fresh manner precisely what needs to be said. I cherish the little triumphs of craft—being able to hold a thought in place until I've found the right way to express it; being able to advance plot through dialogue; to reveal a character by what he says and does, not by what I tell about him; being able to set a scene while something is happening in it. But I also consider my readers collaborators who don't need an overabundance of detail. It is another kind of pleasure to publish: the satisfaction of having endured and produced a whole thing, and one to which a publishing house such as Charles Scribner's Sons is committed.

Along about publication date unreality sets in. I identify with the writer. I'm not sure who the author is. Many years ago I was visiting a publisher's home in which stood a piece of driftwood sculpted by nature to greatly resemble a goat's head. My hostess confided to me that within the family it was referred to as "author." I was both outraged and confounded where I suspected flattery was intended. If I had been able to leave, instead of hanging around like a good author, I might have solved the identity problem right then and there. But in that case, I might not have written a book called *A Town of Masks* (1952) in which the hero/villain suffers from an excess of the same problem: she cannot set her own worth independent of the imagined disdain of others. Unless I am in my fiction, where will its truth come from?

I do not always understand reviewers. By which I suppose I'm saying I don't think reviewers always understand me. If I am not praised of late as generally as I once was, it may be that I am not as successful at what I am attempting as I was books ago. Or is it that reviewers have become more perceptive? I somehow doubt that, but I do pay attention. I must credit my critics with being largely honest, if not always wise. I weigh and accept, perhaps grudgingly, that which may be useful, and discard happily what I know to be destructive. Very often adverse criticism goes to craft, and that sounds an alarm to which attention should be paid. I would seem to be saying that I turn the reviewers over to the writer in me. Let's say I try to. But the author lurks nearby—sorting Band-Aids to fit the wound.

And how do I see myself as seen by my readers? I don't. I simply don't. I know they are there and I am here. I respect and trust them as partners in the fiction. When invited I go among them. I talk about myself, most often about the sources of my writing. But I am at home—I am real to myself—in give-and-take with my audience. Ask me a question concerning me *or* you and I know instantly where and who I am: I am you and you are me, which, I suppose, takes the curse off being me alone up there. I answer letters. I like to receive them even though I open them with a certain trepidation—"Is that what they taught you in the sisters' school?" "In the next printing you might want to correct..."—something carefully researched and still got wrong. And I have never fully recovered from a letter that glowed with praise for *A Gentle Murderer* (1951) and wound up, "Would God there were more Tim Brandons in the world." Tim Brandon being the gentle murderer.

I don't know what I'd have done without the public librarians. I thrive as a writer on library sales. To me this suggests, rightly or wrongly, a selective audience, readers who can ask for and get the authors they want to read. It suggests an informed recommendation. It also suggests a longer shelf life for the books. Some of my nicest letters come from people who have just read, say, my tenth book back. Which brings to mind something Mary Lavin, that lovely Irish writer, said to me once: "When people tell you how much they liked your early books, what it means is they haven't read you since."

I don't write for an audience and I may have already said

why: I cannot see myself from my reader's point of view. If any of my books had brought a disproportionate amount of mail, I think I would have heeded it and tried to follow in my own footsteps the next time round. I have twice launched a series character, once in the late 1950s with Mrs. Norris, the Scottish housekeeper of a retired general and his politician son, and currently with Julie Hayes, who in her fourth book reluctantly settles into the profession of gossip columnist. The first "Julie" book happened because I needed to shake myself up, and I suppose I wanted to earn back a few of the dollars invested in psychotherapy. A therapist figures strongly in *A Death in The Life* (1976): she is likable and a good ballast to Julie. I may have wanted to earn back a few dollars, but the larger truth is I needed to know that I *could* write a therapist. If Julie is to survive, she must grow—from a flaky ne'er-do-well, married to a father figure, into a woman able to support herself. I contemplate that combination of words and wonder what it tells of my peculiar talents. How long has it been since the word "ne'er-do-well" appeared in the language of the day?

Mrs. Norris was retired prematurely, I thought, on my editor's advice, after her third appearance. I had made the mistake of taking up the earlier career of the general who died in the first book of the series, *Death of an Old Sinner* (1957). I ought to have known the perils of resurrection. And no one mourned at the old gentleman's grave more enthusiastically than Mrs. Norris. She deserved to live out a life of her own. The middle book—without the general—is one of my best, *A Gentleman Called* (1958).

Nor do I seem to be able to write to the fashion of the times. Not because I don't want to—I have tried—but because I cannot. I do those obligatory things badly—the spurt of violence, the thrust of sex at regulated intervals. Sometimes I think I'd like to try for an American version of the English "cozy," a hand-me-down from the Golden Age of the detective story. The Mrs. Norris books came close. But that's not where I am. I'm betwixt and between, as my mother used to say, and I'm there for reasons imbedded in my life. Meanwhile, I do write for an audience—of one: myself. I invite everybody in, but I can't complain if they don't all come.

To the question of how I came to write crime fiction I have given many answers, most of them honest at the time of answering. What would seem to me the most ruthlessly honest version at this retrospective is that it seemed to me the only possible thing I could write. And I did want to write. Oh, yes. From the age of two and a half, when I went to work on the wallpaper with a black crayon.

Sometimes I think the main difference between those who write and those who don't, although they'd like to, is the ability to get from here to there, to generate that combustion by which a story moves forward. There is a ruminative fiction I admire which has its own inner dynamics, a movement felt rather than observed; and having had some pretensions early on I might have wanted to go that way, but my ego simply would not provide for the journey. My perception of the dramatic was flawed, but my feeling for the melodramatic was well developed.

But there is more to my becoming a mystery writer than that. When I married I left the Catholic Church. The bonds had already weakened and I would not ask my husband-to-be to convert. Nor do I think he would have even considered it. In marrying Harry Davis, an actor and a Jew, and leaving Chicago for New York, I awakened to a culture utterly alien, deeply enriching, and in time liberating. With Harry's encouragement, I began to write in earnest. But whose was to be the voice? What material? Certainly not my own, which was temporarily in chaos. I started with a story Harry told me of a painter he met in the army who had won a prize in Austria only to have the painting marked for acquisition by the Nazis. He destroyed the painting and ran. He wound up in the illiterate battalion of the United States Army, from which Harry was instrumental in rescuing him. I wrote it as straight suspense. I never finished it, but it got me to an agent and into another book in which paintings were involved and to a locale with which I was more familiar, a small town in the Midwest. When Burroughs Mitchell at Scribners said he liked *The Judas Cat* (1949), but that the denouement was wrong, I agreed with him and said that I could fix it. I then went home and looked up the word denouement. A long time ago I told Dorothy B. Hughes I decided on the mystery because I didn't want to write about myself. "And then went ahead and did it," she said. Quite true. But at a remove— a requisite, I think, to the writing of good fiction.

I realize that in these last paragraphs I may seem to denigrate crime fiction, or worse, to place myself above it. I am where I belong. Rex Stout once said he turned to the mystery when he realized he was not going to write the Great American Novel. I like that. I've had a go at historical and other fiction published outside the crime category, but my technique at its best has always been that of a mystery writer.

A writer whom I don't greatly like but to whom I may well owe the most is Ernest Hemingway. His artistry in evolving plot out of people, action within dialogue, is for me the ideal in storytelling. I admire his leanness. I so admire economy that I am sometimes accused of not finishing a book. But long-winded explanations can spoil a book by calling attention to little things that could have been tied up along the way. Or left untied (to the purist's distress, but not to mine). The sooner I can cut bait among the red herrings the better.

In the late 1940s, when I started, the writer who was doing what I hoped I could one day do was Dorothy B. Hughes. I read and reread *The Fallen Sparrow*, *The Delicate Ape*, *Ride the Pink Horse*. Her social awareness, the urgency of her theme, always integral to the plot, pointed the way I wanted to go. I admired all those Golden Age people: Allingham,

Blake, Carr, Christie, Marsh, Innes, and above all, Dorothy
L. Sayers. It was another world, a nice place to visit, but I
didn't want to live there. Nor could I identify with the giants
of the detective story in America: Hammett, Chandler, Queen,
Stout. I owe something to the influence of Cornell Woolrich.
Mostly in the uses of atmosphere—the ordinary turning ee-
rie, the poison in a perfect apple, an ominous serenity. I felt
the presence of Poe in Woolrich more than in any other
writer. Over the long pull my most admired writer in the
field is Georges Simenon. If ever a writer could make me
believe that black was white it is he; not for an instant would
I doubt the belief of a Simenon character who said that it
was so. I wish I could write a Maigret. I so identify with the
aging inspector I feel chilled to the bone when he puts his
feet out of bed onto the cold flagstones in the gray light of
dawn. I can even identify with Madame Maigret, and that's
pretty excessive.

There is one crime novel I cherish above all others, *Brighton
Rock* by Graham Greene. By and large, I'd rather read about
sin than evil. I agree with Flannery O'Connor that it is more
interesting. But for pure evil, the boy Pinkie in *Brighton Rock*
has no equal. Dorian Grey is a pussycat. And the amiable,
sensual, port-loving Ida, who becomes the pursued man's
shield, is a beautifully counterpointed character. Unforget-
table. All of Graham Greene's work is important to me. I
share his human concerns and, generally speaking, his political views as I understand them. I do sometimes bridle at
his passive women and ugly Americans. But I follow him
closely in the recurring theme of man's struggle with and for
religious faith.

It has been said that I have "carved a particularly relevant
niche in the genre in the melding of crises of faith into the
suspense novel." I do feel that my best crime books hinge
on religious conflicts, probably because it is the area of my
deepest insights. After saying that, and having embraced the

reviewer's accolade right off, I have just reexamined the premise and must qualify: my best books concern human sexuality in conflict with the strictures of the Church. Which certainly positions the books more interestingly. A crisis of faith without sin, sex, or guilt wouldn't stand much chance in crime fiction.

A Gentle Murderer (1951) is generally considered my best book. If a classic is a book that is rarely out of print, then it belongs among the notable. It has been reprinted by six different publishers and is scheduled to appear next year in the Bantam Mystery Classics. It is the story of a killer who would be a holy man and the young girl who idolizes him— as he does her—and the girl's widowed mother who would simply have him in her bed; he has killed before under such pressure. A detective knows it, a priest suspects it. But where is he? The book opens and closes with the words, "Bless me, Father, for I have sinned...." And the reader is left with a kind of grief, the feeling of "If only...."

Another book with the same blend is *God Speed the Night* (1968) written with Jerome Ross. It is set in Occupied France during World War II. In it is my favorite of my villains, Moissac, an anti-Semitic police officer, deeply religious, who forgives himself his lust, assuming that the young woman he wants is Jewish. Someone commented to me of Moissac, "The poor bastard," and I knew I had done him well. It is almost superfluous to say I often treasure my villains more than my heroes.

That is not the case, however, with *Where the Dark Streets Go* (1969). This is my favorite of my own books and Father Joseph McMahon is my best hero. As nearly as I can tell the book started with a question I had jotted down in my journal some time before: "We know what a priest is to others, but what is he to himself?" Ideas, long dormant or even kicked around and abandoned, have a way of rising again when the need is at hand. It was the time of the Vietnam War and flower children and a changing Church. I was, of all things, feeling nostalgic for a beloved tyrant. The book with, again, a New York setting, opens on the last few minutes in the life of an unknown man, a victim of assault, who challenges the faith of the priest who comes to help him. In seeking to learn first who the man was and then why he died as he did, the priest finds himself—or loses himself—depending on the reader's bent.

It is curious, the uses to which we put our themes—or divert them. I had thought at first to write a story of a young man who steals a suitcase and discovers in it the clerical suit, bib, and collar of a priest, as well as his breviary. In fact, I did use that incident in *The Little Brothers* (1973). But what I had originally intended to do with it was to grace and turn the boy around with the discovery and set him on a career of good deeds, disguising himself as a priest. I foresaw him coming to believe he was a priest. Counterpoint to his story was to be that of the priest, on the verge of dropping out at the time when the manifest trappings of his identity were stolen. I envisioned a murder in there somewhere that would involve them both. Perhaps the boy was to become violent when his priesthood was challenged. I suspect what put me off the entire gambit was my husband's appearance about that time in a zany film, *The Gang Who Couldn't Shoot Straight*, in which Robert de Niro spent a lot of footage disguised as a priest. How strange that these few years later my story is hardly viable because the Catholic clergy are out of their traditional garb so much of the time. Does it become viable again if Pope John Paul gets them back into the habit? Then one is tempted to question the relevance of the subject in the first place. Given the monstrous material available to the crime writer in my writing lifetime, what kind of impact can I hope to make with a kid playing priest on the streets of New York? Ah, but the theme is bigger than it seems, and insight rides with the viewer as well as with the exhibitor.

I was driving alone in Spain during the last years of Franco when two enormous and tough-looking Civil Guards stopped me and wrote out a summons. I had no idea what offense I was charged with, nor could they cross the language barrier to explain, nor did I think they tried. What they easily made clear was that I was to pay the fine to them. Which I did on the spot. Then, as I understood it, I was to appear in court in Tarragona, some fifty miles away. We communicated badly, to say the least, but I sensed no feeling of need on their part to communicate at all. On the road to Tarragona I felt stricken with a great illumination: those men were little Francos to themselves: uniforms, helmets, and a modicum of Franco's power given into their hands. I understood at last how dictators maintained power: they shared it. It only somewhat dimmed my illumination presently to admit that I could have crossed the double lines on that perilously winding road and to learn that the guards had allowed me to pay the fine then and there so that I would not have to interrupt my journey unless I wished to deny the offense in court in Tarragona. I've had some useful misapprehensions in my day.

The crime novel is more reflective of its own time and more confined within it, I think, than other kinds of fiction. A benefit is in its feeling of immediacy, and generally speaking, those books which survive do so not only because they are well written, but because they are steeped in the mores, the tempo, and the urgent concerns of the time in which they were written. I think all time capsules should contain a crime fiction of the day.

However, the prevailing framework within which the crime writer must fashion his fiction—even if his story is aimed at breaking down that framework—is law and order, the conserving of the peace. In that context I do see crime fiction as inherently conservative. Which is not to say a radical hero— or an antihero, if you will—cannot operate within the medium. His success will depend on the writer's performance *and* the predilection of all those readers out there, the majority of whom at this writing is undoubtedly conservative.

I don't think crime writers as a whole are politically conservative, although I do think that even as with the readership, a majority may lean that way today. I know that when I came into the field in the late 1940s the trend was quite the other way except, notably, among those tarriers in the Golden Age. We were aware of the Great Depression and the War and all the issues growing out of it. We were aware of the death camps. Crime fiction concerned with "the mean streets" had come to the fore. We were in the vanguard of change, of moving a bizarre fiction into the world around us. I think of writers like Charlotte Armstrong, Stanley Ellin, Andrew Garve, Patricia Highsmith, Ross Macdonald, Margaret Millar.

The giants of the Golden Age may have created in their fiction a world that never was, but it represented a highly structured order, which is why murder in the vicar's garden is so horrid. And so delicious. That there is such nostalgia today for those graceful monuments to class and prejudice says much about the anxiety of our times.

I don't think anyone could read two or three of my books without knowing that I am a liberal. It might even take no more than a few paragraphs. A liberal with a strong conservative streak down the middle. I'm one of those "Mother, I'd rather do it myself" people. As I've indicated earlier, I have trouble with heroes. I think this means that I am less interested in characters who reflect my point of view than in those who challenge it. And what it would probably be more accurate to say is that I can do well enough with heroes who change in the progress of a book. There we have it: it's those fixed stars that I've had trouble with—the police detective and my early virginal heroines who were too good to be true and weren't. I still believe in goodness. I'm just more careful about where I go to look for it.

Since I feel so strongly that a writer's best material is one's self, I look to my childhood for the earliest sources of my fiction. My mother was a North of Ireland Catholic, my father, born in England—in Thomas Hardy country—a convert and more Catholic than the Pope. Than my mother, certainly. We moved from Chicago to northern Wisconsin when I was six. My father loved the farm; my mother hated it, even though she was a recluse. He was a joiner. He'd wanted a boy; they settled for me. I too loved the farm. Every animal was my best friend. I could milk cows when I was seven and drove a tractor at ten. I rode bareback anything with legs. Meanwhile, my mother was making very modest progress in trying to raise a little lady. (I came round along about adolescence.)

My father read aloud to us after supper. His favorite stories were about Indians and no doubt cowboys. I think he related them to his own experience as a cavalryman fighting the Filipino guerrillas after Spain ceded the Islands to the United States in 1898. His own stories are as vivid to me today as they were when he told them—the ambushes and massacres, the fears and heroism of young soldiers untrained for that kind of warfare. My father was never the hero, but his horse often was. My mother's stories were mostly melancholic, full of a deep longing for *home*. Her language was rich, the images often cruel: My heart's scalded... Happy as a goat a-hanging... It'd melt the heart of a wheelbarrow... You can get used to anything, even hanging if you hang long enough... And when I'd ask what was for supper: Sweeps' heels and roasted snow. I worked that image out for myself reading Hans Christian Andersen.

The first Christmas I remember clearly was in the wilds of Wisconsin, to use my mother's words. She and I plunged our way through the snow and found a tree. My father chopped it down for us. We decorated it with illustrations we cut out of the color section of the Sears Roebuck catalogue.

I remember that winter my father bringing in a gunnysack full of fish he'd caught through a hole cut in the lake ice. He emptied it on the kitchen floor for sorting. Afterward, every once in a while fish scales would glisten in the lamplight like sequins between the floorboards. The first two years of my formal education were spent in a one-room schoolhouse with a single teacher to attend all grades. I doubt that I was ever again as thoroughly educated in a similar amount of time. I sped through my assignments while others were having arithmetic and so could pay attention to everybody's history and geography lessons: their reading was too slow for me and I was considered a showoff from Chicago. Miss Darling, the teacher, didn't help my status a bit by having me read the eighth grade's "Evangeline" aloud to the entire school—all fourteen pupils.

When I gained access to a public library with our move back to Illinois in the middle twenties, I read everything I could find by Robert Louis Stevenson, Zane Grey, and Louisa May Alcott. I don't know how to account for it today, but in high school I was passionate about Sir Walter Scott and George Eliot. I gobbled Hawthorne, Irving, and Poe. Had trouble with Melville and Conrad. I still do. And I shall never get to the top of *The Magic Mountain*. I discovered the French in college, then the Russians. I made my own charts of their names. I back up to when I was twelve or so, having just read a book of famous dog stories. I coaxed our Airedale upstairs with me and onto my bed. When my mother came to make sure I wasn't reading by flashlight under the blanket, Jock bared his teeth and growled at her. Never did an indoor dog convert to an outdoor dog so fast.

My father was a conservative Democrat. He wore a brown derby when Al Smith was running for president, which his buddies stole from him at the American Legion Hall. Al Smith wasn't really popular in Lake Forest, Illinois. My mother was outraged when my father deigned to step into the hall again afterward. He was hurt, but he contended it was his place, too. I suspect he gained a certain esteem among his colleagues for his lonely stand. Needless to say, I grew up standing with him. Until the era of Father Coughlin. After my first vote for Roosevelt and my father's last vote for him, I don't think we were ever in the same political camp again. But to this day I can cross over and make a pretty good argument for the opposition.

There had been another cross-over in my life although I did not know about it until I was seventeen. I was allowed to do some emergency banking for my father which required papers out of the safety-deposit box. Alone in the bank vault, rifling through the box, I came on my baptismal certificate and learned that I'd been adopted at the age of one. It was a year before I told my adoptive parents that I knew, and it was only last year, about fifty years later, that I obtained a court order and opened my original birth record in Spring-field, Illinois. There is a detective story in the making: a twin, of all things.

My mother died when I was twenty and my father soon remarried, but by then I had left the farm for good. Those of us who grew up during the Great Depression are different, I swear. Perhaps it came of an awareness of others either more fortunate or unfortunate than ourselves—or in the same boat. The point is that we were aware of one another to an extraordinary degree. It was a time of hope, really, when people felt they had to—and eventually that they could—do something. And I think that with the assorted projects provided by the government, whether the work was with the pen or the pickax, the participants came to see them-selves as learners, as men and women with heads as well as stomachs. If I have bespoken the liberal in me, here is the conservative: the summer after I finished college I worked on Historical Research in the Waukegan, Illinois, county courthouse. It was a Federal Writers Project offshoot. I finished in a month work that was supposed to take me three, and when I was sent back to find something in the dusty files to occupy me till fall, I quit the project. The WPA wasn't the place for overachievers. Nevertheless.

The only job I could find for some time afterward was traveling small-town America promoting a magic show. It was the loneliest if, as eventually proved out, the most provident period of my life. So much of my fiction has roots in coal dust and the prairie.

I like best to read biography and history. And often poetry, which, with a small group of friends, Harry and I read aloud. I reread Faulkner, Flannery O'Connor, Malcolm Lowry. I'm not well up on contemporary fiction outside the crime perimeters. Within them I read everything by Lionel Davidson, Joseph Hansen, P. D. James, Patrick McGinley, Ruth Rendell, and Donald E. Westlake...and numerous of the younger writers who seem to come up out of nowhere and to be going everywhere. That, I feel, is the splendid state of crime fiction today: it has no limits on where it can go, no proscription on how it can get there. The growth of a writer like Dick Francis is stunning.

I regret the temporary, partial eclipse of police-procedurals. I admire and learn from Ed McBain, Michael Gilbert, Hillary Waugh. And in among them must be named a writer almost forgotten, and most undeservedly—the late Maurice Procter, a Yorkshire constable who wrote during the 1950s and 1960s with an authentic regional voice so clear it touched the universe. I've not mentioned two favorites, Eric Ambler, simply a master, and Josephine Tey. Whatever prejudice I bring to reading writers of the Golden Age and their inheritors, Tey overcomes it. She has humor and she is wise, and it is too bad she did not live to write more plays and more than those eight crime novels.

I am pleased that Academe has seen fit to bestow on crime fiction even a qualified legitimacy. I'm sure the weight won't sink it. I don't really know what "popular culture" means, and I'm not sure culture of any sort is popular just now. Does it mean culture for the masses? Or a frivolous fiction for the elite? Gymnastics for the intellectual? I'm sure crime fiction can be all these things. And sometimes, unselfconsciously, literature.

I hope people who study its forms in order to write it will come to it with the pure intention of learning how best to tell the story they need to tell. There is no "best" way except that in which the writer is at his best. I say to myself time and again: stay simple. Simenon wouldn't have to say it at all. And I very much doubt that Deighton or Le Carré would. Each to his own fiction. It will find its audience.

Quantity and Quality

Michael Gilbert

Some years ago I wrote a fairly light-hearted piece for the *Mystery Writers Handbook*, edited by Herbert Brean. I invented for it a word, "technicalese," which I defined as the superficial use of acquired techniques to adorn a story.

The point I was making—not a very subtle one—was that the routine of a detective story, involving certain almost obligatory characters—murderer, murderee, and detective—would be apt to become tedious with repetition, but that the tedium could be alleviated by choosing different and colorful backgrounds for each book.

I pointed out that no personal knowledge of these backgrounds was necessary. There are shelves full of excellent books of reference in most public libraries. "You contemplate the murder of a Javanese cult-dancer with a guillotine: but certainly. See under Exploration, Eurythmics and Penology."

Rereading this article recently, my eye was caught by the warning which I inserted at the end of it on the subject of detail. I suggested that while the writer could be fancy-free about the picturesque details which he flung into his background, he *must* be accurate if any of those details affected the plot. Because when this happens they cease to be technicalese and become technique. Quite a different matter.

At this point it occurred to me that I was playing round on the outskirts of a problem which can affect all crime writers. It is, in fact, a double problem. First, the extent to which detailed description of people, places, and procedures helps, or hinders, a crime story; and secondly, the allied question of when accuracy of detail is necessary and when it is not.

Before plunging into it, a preliminary point of definition must be settled.

Anyone who has studied the genre will appreciate that there are at least two distinct forms of crime writing. Some have subdivided even further. Anthony Boucher, whose expertise no one would question, finds five categories. The puzzle, the whodunit, the hard-boiled novel, the pursuit novel, and the straight novel of character analysis. An arrangement which I find simpler to handle is to amalgamate the puzzle and the whodunit and refer to them as "detective stories," and the hard-boiled and pursuit stories and call them "thrillers." (The fifth really defies classification.)

There is a fundamental reason for keeping detective stories and thrillers in a different critical pocket. True, they both set out to entertain the reader. If they did not, they would hardly be written and would certainly not be read. But they set about it in quite a different way.

The detective story entertains by intriguing, by setting the reader a puzzle which he can try to solve if he feels so inclined, and by presenting him with a neat solution which he had never thought of but which, on reflection, he can accept as being logical.

Ronald Knox summed it up when he said that the ideal detective story was one you could read in bed, and end by kicking yourself, under the bedclothes, for not having outsmarted the author.

The object of the thriller, on the other hand, is to thrill, to excite, to alarm, even to shock. Expressions traditionally associated with such reading—"It made my flesh creep; my hair stand on end; my blood run cold" are all more or less accurate medical descriptions of the effect of shock.

Now it is no part of my purpose to argue about whether the detective story or the thriller is the higher form of writing. Raymond Chandler pulverized the detective story in his well-known polemic "The Simple Art of Murder," which first appeared in the *Atlantic Monthly* in 1944 and has been often reprinted. Professor Jacques Barzun, in a less widely known but equally effective article in *Holiday*, put the thriller in its place and restored the detective story to its pedestal.

I have tried my hand at both and can only repeat here what I am on record as saying a number of times before, that the thriller is more difficult to bring off than the detective story. Much more difficult. I first brashly produced this dictum in the premises of the Detection Club when I was a newly elected member of that distinguished fraternity of crime writers. It may surprise you to know that it received the emphatic support of Dorothy Sayers.

My object in keeping the two types separate is to see whether the problem of detailed description differs according to which sort of book you are writing. S. S. Van Dine, the author of the Philo Vance stories, had no doubts about the matter: "A detective novel should contain no long descriptive passages, no literary dallying with side-issues, no subtly worked-out character analyses, no atmospheric pre-occupations. Such matters have no vital place in a record of crime and deduction."

This dictum by a man little read today, but a phenomenal best seller in his own lifetime, is worth studying almost word by word: and I shall return to it more than once. For the moment, it is a relief to see that Anthony Boucher, who quotes it, concludes: "What was, in 1928, a commercially valid rule for mystery writing has now become a precise recipe of how *not* to write a mystery—if you hope to get it published."

Which is just as well, because construed literally it reduces the problem to the type—"If A can do a job in three days, B in four days, and C in five days, how many days will it take them to do it working together?" If asked to solve it (and it is curiously difficult for a nonmathematician), you might wish to be told that A, B, and C were reliable types and would continue to work at precisely the same pace when together, and not stop to gossip; on the other hand, you would be justifiably irritated if the additional information was thrown in that A was homosexual, B a masochist, and that C suffered from an Oedipus complex.

A measure, then, of helpful description is permissible, but how much, and how detailed? And is the proportion different in detective stories and thrillers?

Take people first. (And before I am accused of being a male chauvinist, may I say that I fully recognize that characters can be of both sexes. It is simply that, in writing, I find the constant repetition of "he or she" tiresome. I prefer to adopt the note which I found at the head of a legal document: "Throughout the following, the male embraces the female.") To proceed.

Certain guidelines in character drawing seem to be accepted by most fiction writers today. They do not now blatantly assert the accomplishments of their characters. The days of "You know X, one of the two most dangerous men in Europe" are happily past. The modern rule is the Biblical one. "By their fruits shall ye know them."

It was not always so. Edgar Allan Poe, introducing us to that remarkable man C. Auguste Dupin, kicks off with four formidable paragraphs:

"The mental features discoursed of as the analytical are but little susceptible of analysis."

"The faculty of resolution is possibly much invigorated by mathematical study."

"Whist has long been noted for its influence upon the calculating power."

"The analytical power should not be confounded with simple ingenuity."

You realize that I am only giving you the opening sentences of the four paragraphs, none of them short and one covering more than fifty lines of print, a dissertation on analytical ability which Agatha Christie managed to compress into three words by a reference to Poirot's "little grey cells."

Equally, it is possible and agreeable to the lazy reader (by which I mean the majority of readers) to describe a man's character by what he says. As a critic commented about Dirk Bogarde (a film star and also an excellent writer), his figures reveal themselves, sharp as glass in every syllable they utter.

If, then, these methods of indirect description are adopted, is there anything left about a character which needs actual description? Clearly, only his personal appearance.

"He was worth looking at. He wore a shaggy borsalino hat, a rough grey sports coat with white golf balls on it for buttons, a brown shirt, a yellow tie, pleated grey flannel slacks and alligator shoes with white explosion on the toes. From his outer breast pocket cascaded a show handkerchief of the same brilliant yellow as his tie. There were a couple of coloured feathers tucked into the band of his hat."

So much for his clothes. We turn to his physical attributes: .

"He was a big man, but not more than six foot five inches tall and not wider than a beer truck. His skin was pale and he needed a shave. He had curly black hair and heavy eyebrows that almost met over his thick nose. His ears were small and neat for a man of that size and his eyes had a shine close to tears that grey eyes often seem to have." That was Raymond Chandler in *Farewell My Lovely*.

It's a long description, and yet not a syllable too long for the perceptive reader. To him it is like the introductory chords in a piece of music which lead up to a sudden sforzando. He knows that the man so particularly placed before him is soon going to be involved in violent action.

Now compare this with the description of Jessica Palinode in *More Work for the Undertaker* by Margery Allingham. "Her small squat form was arrayed in an assortment of garments of varying length, and as she sat with her knees crossed she revealed a swag of multi-coloured hems festooned across a concertina'd stocking. At that distance her shoes appeared to be stuffed with grass. Wisps of it sprouted from every aperture, including one at the toe. It was warm in the sun but she wore across her shoulders something which might once have been a fur and her elf-locks peeped out from under the yellowing folds of an ancient motoring veil of the button-on-top variety. Since she wore it over a roughly torn square of cardboard placed flat on her head the effect was eccentric and even pathetic."

Agreed that Margery Allingham's description is, in its quieter way, as effective as Chandler's. But it has got into the wrong book. If it had been in one of her thrillers (and she wrote a number of excellent thrillers), the reader would have swallowed it whole. Knowing that something exciting was going to happen to the old freak, and soon. She was due to be mugged or murdered, or maybe she was a policewoman in disguise. Not so in the sober ritual of a detective story. Our next meeting with Jessica is six chapters later, when she is found, at three o'clock in the morning, brewing nettle tea in the kitchen: by which time the patient reader, if he remembers her at all, will certainly have forgotten what she looked like.

"In detective stories," said Van Dine, "no long descriptive passages," and "No subtly worked-out character analyses." Here he has a supporter in Barzun: "I pick up Mary Kelly's *Dead Man's Riddle*, a story laid in a Scottish university. The problem: murder and forgery. Excellent, but why in the name of literature must I be fobbed off with long discussions of the detective's problems. Am I a couch?"

It is clear that Barzun, too, is discussing a detective story.

Neither he nor Van Dine, be it noted, condemns detailed personal description and psychological insights in a thriller.

Very well. If it be so—and accept it for the sake of argument—that a thriller can sustain and benefit from long and detailed descriptions of its puppets and places while similar treatment is out of place in a detective story, is there some reason which stems from the inherent differences between the two? I think there is. And I think that the explanation goes some way toward explaining the different degree of difficulty which faces the authors of these two very different types of book.

The reading of any work of fiction demands a surrender by the reader. Only the very young believe that all that appears between the covers of a book is true. Quite soon they realize that the words on the page are spelling out a series of lies. If they are thoughtful infants, they may be puzzled by the effect which these untruths produce. They are told by their father that a certain book "should not be read after dark. It is too frightening." They may even see tears in their mother's eyes as she reads. How can words which they know are not true affect people in such ways?

They soon discover that all that is necessary is for them to make a surrender to the author. Once Alice has fallen down the rabbit hole and landed safely on her feet, the Mock Turtle, the White Knight, and the Red Queen *become* real.

That is an example of an initial act of surrender. And it is an act which everyone performs when he opens the pages of a detective story. He is being asked to accept a world which is every bit as strange, in its way, as Alice's Wonderland. It is a world in which a murder can be solved cerebrally; a world in which the solution can be produced by a private person taking thought. While he very well knows, in his rational mind, that murders are solved by teams of police officers, and that they are not solved by taking thought but by taking statements.

In the *Mystery Writers Handbook* the matter is very clearly expressed by Lawrence Treat, in his article on the Real Life Policeman. "The private eye is really a modern-day Don Quixote unrolled from the romantic dreams of childhood. He is Peter Pan dressed in mundane clothing. He is fable mixed with fact. Once this concept is clear, the writer can carry it forward in his own particular way. *The sin to be avoided is to imply true-to-lifeness.*"

The italics in the last sentence are mine, because here, I think, Treat puts his finger precisely on the point. Once the writer has invited the reader to step into the fantasy world of the detective story it is not only a mistake, it is positively destructive, to make repeated attempts to persuade the reader that the world he has entered is a real one.

On the introductory page of *More Work for the Undertaker*, Margery Allingham writes: "Every character in this book is a careful portrait of a living person." In other words, she confesses at the outset that she has committed the very sin that Lawrence Treat warned against. There is much in it of wit and good writing but the book is blemished, as Alice in Wonderland would have been blemished had her mother shouted, from time to time, down the rabbit hole: "Don't be alarmed, darling: It's only a dream. A real turtle is far more interesting than a mock turtle."

In the case of the thriller, the situation is very different. The reader is not in an imaginary world. He is in a world which, alas, he knows well: a world of violence, of treachery, and of all-too-possible sorrow.

The job of the writer is first to delineate a section of this world in credible colors and then to think up a plausible reason for introducing his hero (to use an old-fashioned word—antihero is sometimes more apt) to this particular scene.

If the hero is a policeman or an intelligence operative, no problem. He will be ordered to do the job. Or he will be ordered not to do it, but will defy orders because his pal (his girl) has been liquidated (raped) by the opposition. Either way he is plausibly in the ring and fighting with both hands.

With a private citizen it is more difficult. At one time it was possible to create a character like Bulldog Drummond who was bored and unhappy when he was not having a bash at Carl Peterson. The more sophisticated readers of today will not accept this. If a man goes round looking for trouble he is not a hero. He's plain stupid, and the one thing a thriller writer must never do is to allow his reader to snigger. In fact he must scarcely allow the reader time to draw breath. He must be made to believe so implicitly in the reality of hero and villain that the struggle between them becomes his own struggle.

When it comes to description, the hero requires less than the villain. The hero is essentially the reader. All he needs is a name to identify him. Sometimes he doesn't even get that. All that we know about the Continental Op after two full-length novels and a dozen short stories is that he is short, thickset, and balding, and the narrator of Len Deighton's first four books is even more sparsely dealt with. He is not only not described, he hadn't even a name until he reached the screen, and then we could see him and no description was necessary.

Not so with villains. They have to be handled with much greater care. In his earlier books, Ian Fleming was conscious of this and devoted thought and skill to building them up. Consider the two nasties in *From Russia With Love*, the unspeakable female director of the Russian terror organization Smersh ("squat and toadlike") and the professional killer who carried out her missions. When we first meet him he is lying nearly naked, face downward so that we can admire his deltoid muscles and his triceps, and a long passage devoted to physical description is followed by a chapter describing his youth and upbringing. It was after this book that a critic commented that although Bond was not killed he was never quite the same man again. But it was not Bond who had deteriorated. It was the plausibility of his villains.

As with people, so with things.

"No atmospheric preoccupations," said Van Dine. Without clarifying exactly what he meant, this prohibition would clearly limit evocative descriptions of places.

In a detective story the description of a place has a functional significance. It is part of the plot. In early examples of the genre it was not unusual for the author to supplement his verbal description with a sketch map of the neighborhood along with a more detailed plan of the summerhouse, library, or bedroom where the body was found. When unassisted by a plan it was nonetheless essential for the reader to follow closely the description that was offered. If he failed to appreciate that the mirror in Simon Harlowe's Treasure Room was directly opposite the clock he would have missed one of the essential points in A. E. W. Mason's *The House of the Arrow*, which is, along with *At the Villa Rose* and *The Prisoner in the Opal*, the best of the Hanaud stories.

It should be added that although all three are detective stories, in that the mainspring of each is a murder and the unmasking of the murderer, Mason was too essentially a novelist to construct any of them on the strict lines of a "whodunit." He engrafts plenty of excitements, and it is the existence of such hybrids that makes hard and fast generalizations about the two types of book more difficult.

One thing, however, stands out. It is only in the thriller that evocative descriptions can be ridden on a loose rein. I wrote, in another place, that "the detective story is the sonnet. It is precise, neat, and satisfyingly symmetrical. The thriller is the ode. It has no formal rules. It has no precise framework. It has no top, and, heaven knows, no bottom." It is because of this shapelessness that the wildest fancies and "atmospheric preoccupations" find a place in it.

To illustrate the point I had intended to quote the well-known passage in Chandler's *The High Window* in which he describes Bunker Hill ("old town, lost town, shabby town, crook town...") but I decided that in this case it would be appropriate if the passage came from the author whom Julian Symons has described as "the poet of the spy story," though I am aware that the book it comes from, *The Billion Dollar Brain*, gets a sharp rap from Barzun and Taylor in their *Catalogue of Crime*, as containing "many boring stretches."

"Five o'clock is the top dead centre of the Manhattan night. Just for one hour the city is inert. The hearses have been brought up to the doors of the city hospitals, but they haven't yet begun to unload. The last cinema on Forty-Second street has closed and even the billiard rooms have racked the cues and shut down. The last wino has curled into newspaper and stretched out on the last bench in Battery Park. Down in Washington Produce Market they are huddled round the oil-drum fires. It is so cold even muggers have stayed at home, to the regret of the patrolmen longing to thaw their ears in the Precinct House. The city's seventy thousand wild cats have pounced upon pigeons in Riverside Park or Norwegian wharf rats in Washington Market and now they too are asleep under the long lines of still cars. The only movement is compressed steam roaring along at three hundred miles an hour under the roadways, escaping now and again with a spectral puff, and the shuffle of wet newspapers as far as the eye can see down the long long streets to the bloodshot dawn."

You have to make up your own mind about a passage like that. Actually I have left out three sections of it. In the original it fills a complete page. This could be one of the "boring stretches" deplored by Barzun and Taylor. I can only record that I found it superbly evocative; maybe that's because I evoke easily.

Certain things about it, however, are clear. It has no structural connection with the story. Nothing turns on the absence of the patrolmen from the precinct house or the fate of the pigeons and the wharf rats. The action which follows takes place in another part of New York altogether, in General Midwinter's private apartment (also amply described) on the fiftieth floor of an office block in Wall Street.

The other thing which is clear about it is that it would have been signally out of place in a detective story.

So far we have been examining the proportion of descriptive to narrative passages and the extent to which, in different types of book, they can carry a superstructure of detail.

The accuracy of that detail is another matter altogether.

Whatever sort of book you are writing—detective story, thriller, police procedural, or spy story—it is, of course, preferable to be accurate. The important matter here is not the nature of the book; it is the nature of the inaccuracy.

A few examples from the extensive list which can be compiled from my own works may make this point clearer.

In an early book I placed two of my characters on the wrong branch of the Northern (tube) Line. The precise branch they were on was not a matter of any importance. So far as the plot was concerned it could have been any line leading to any destination. I have never received more, nor more virulent, letters of complaint. You might have thought that I was deliberately setting out to get my readers onto the wrong train.

If I learned one thing from this it was that a nonfunctional inaccuracy such as this has a drawback. It annoys readers. When my wife was reading Frederick Forsyth's first book, *The Day of the Jackal,* she was so irritated to find a French rural policeman patroling on his own (according to her they *always* work in pairs) that she refused to finish the book, and never discovered whether General de Gaulle was assassinated or not.

So far I have been speaking of nonfunctional inaccuracies, meaning inaccuracies over some detail which is no part of

90

the machinery by which the plot turns. I am not recommending them, unless, as some writers are believed to do, you insert them in order to enter into correspondence with your readers. It is merely that I think they are unimportant.

I have noted a difference here between English and American proofreaders. In America the more peripheral the inaccuracy the more pain it seems to cause. In a recent book I made a reference to something happening on Midsummer Day. From the fact that the next day was a Thursday, it was evident that I was supposing Midsummer Day to have been on a Wednesday that year. And why not? Impossible, said the proofreader. In an earlier passage you have mentioned that the American Third Battle Fleet was stationed off Beirut, and in the year in which that last happened Midsummer Day was a Friday. I capitulated. But I should have been more concerned if the error had been a functional one.

I have been guilty of plenty of those, too.

In the days when I was writing television serials (happy, innocent days of the birth of the box) I concluded one episode with the hero moving across to find out why the canary, in a cage which hung in a corner of his workroom, had died. As he approached it something—I think it must have been the background music—warned him of approaching danger and before opening the metal door of the cage he wrapped a heavy rubber tobacco pouch round his hand. A wise precaution. The cage had been wired to the electric mains and was live. A beautiful flash concluded the episode.

On that occasion I was never quite sure whether I was right or wrong about killing the canary. One of the advantages of writing for television is that most of the angry letters go to the producer. On this occasion I got only one, from a man who signed himself Sherlock Holmes. It said "Watson and I have been discussing the death of that bird. We concluded that it must have died of shock at the author's ignorance of electricity."

A much more important example occurred in one of my

detective stories called "Smallbone Deceased," in which the central point was, as the title implies, the decease of a man called Smallbone. The killer stood behind him as he sat, unsuspecting, in a chair in the office of his solicitor, and slipped over his head a homemade garotte. This had been constructed by taking a length of picture wire, making a hole in it near one end and passing the other end through the hole, forming a loop. A wooden toggle was then attached to each end of the wire to afford a good grip.

My detective, examining the marks on the victim's neck, noticed that the creases in the skin on the right-hand side were deeper than those on the left, and concluded from this that most of the tugging had been done by the killer's left hand. I considered this to be a clever deduction—left-hand killer.

Not so a correspondent who lived in Rome and from whom I received a four-page letter. It was courteously phrased, and started by correcting the spelling of two or three Italian terms which I had used. Then he came to the point. The soundness of the deduction of left-handedness must depend on which end of the wire had the hole in it. He illustrated this with two careful sketches, and I began to feel that he was right. He clinched the matter by saying that he had constructed two models, one each way, and tried them on his wife. Different creases each time, it appears.

If my correspondent was right, and he was the only person who had the support of clinical evidence, then this was a serious inaccuracy, because an important part of the plot turned on it. Nor did the fact of my receiving only one letter absolve me. There may have been any number of others who had detected the same point but had not troubled to write. And this, remember, was a detective story. A thriller may ride roughshod over a few blemishes. When Chandler was asked who killed the chauffeur in his book *The Big Sleep*, after giving the point some thought he said that he didn't really know. The implication was that it didn't really matter. And this was one of his acknowledged masterpieces. In a detective story such casualness would have been as fatal to the plot as to the chauffeur.

Since procedures *are* normally functional to the plot, errors about them are likely to be more serious than errors about things. Two sorts of procedure dominate the crime story: police work, including that branch of the law which deals with criminal matters, and Intelligence organization.

Of the two, the operations of Intelligence offer more latitude to the writer, because no one knows, or is supposed to know, anything about them, and changes are not publicly advertised. In England certain convenient shorthands have outlived actuality for generations. MI5 and MI6 really had, originally, some connection with Military Intelligence, but they are now the concern of the Home Office and the Foreign Office, respectively, while the letter "C" was long used to designate the head of Intelligence on the grounds that at one time the holder of that office was a man called Cumming.

From the writer's point of view, the important thing is not the fact that Intelligence organizations change, but that the average reader's conception of them changes, as fast as new and presumably more up-to-date books are written. Whether this conception becomes more accurate is a moot point; possibly so. The reader certainly becomes more sophisticated and more suspicious of implausible behavior.

Consider the case of Richard Hannay, who worked on two occasions (*Greenmantle* and *Mr. Standfast*) under the orders of Sir Walter Bullivant. In the first of these books, set in the period of the Kaiser's War, Hannay has been dispatched to Germany in the guise of an anti-British Afrikaaner in order to unravel a plot to raise the banner of Islam against the British in the Middle East. Hannay is on the point of doing just this. He is to be dispatched, by the Germans, with excellent credentials, to the place where he can discover all the answers, when the bullying Prussian General Von Stumm makes the mistake of grabbing him by his wounded shoulder. Whereupon Hannay clips him under the jaw and decamps into the middle of the Black Forest in a snowstorm.

When I first read *Greenmantle*, in my school days, I was not in the least upset by this. It seemed to me to be the way in which bullying Prussian generals should be treated, and I had every confidence that Hannay would make his way to Constantinople under his own steam. Subsequently—and I have reread the book at least three times—doubts did begin to creep in, though I should hesitate to say that they spoiled this excellent thriller for me. It was rather that a combination of the fictions of Trevanian, Deighton, and Le Carré, and the facts of Allen Dulles and Sir Paul Dukes, had insensibly changed my views of how a spy would be likely to behave.

It seems therefore that the criterion in espionage stories is not how accurate the procedures are in fact, but how closely they correspond to what the reader believes them to be, a conclusion which can be taken a step further. Spies read spy stories. The cruder efforts may only provoke sardonic laughter, but when a spy chances on an author who either knows, or has made an instructed guess at the sort of problem which might face an intelligence operative, and has displayed some ingenuity in suggesting how it could be solved, might he not be tempted to try something like it himself?

Thus the "dirty tricks" department of fiction merges with the "dirty tricks" of real life. A sobering thought for both parties.

With police procedures in England no such latitude is excusable. If he wishes to be accurate, the writer has only to get hold of a copy of the reference book known as General Orders which specifies every detail of police organization down to such important points as when officers are permitted to wear shirt-sleeves without their tunics and how the sleeves should be rolled.

In America he may be less happily placed. Lawrence Treat says, "There is, unfortunately, no reference book to consult on police department set-ups." However, the criterion in both cases is the same. If the point of procedure is functional, you *must* get it right.

Because both my final examples come from the works of Dorothy Sayers it must not be thought that I am decrying either her or that type of whodunit which is particularly associated with her name. It is a mistake to think that no one nowadays writes or reads detective stories. As Edmund Crispin remarked, "their obsequies have often been pronounced, but they remain obstinately alive," and Julian Symons, replying recently to an author who was complaining that new writers tended to be neglected in the bookshops, said, "The popularity of Christie, Sayers and Marsh is no news to me. As the Penguin adviser on crime stories for five years I know quite well what books sell most copies."

I would like to examine one of Sayers's books and one of her short stories. The story is in a collection originally published in 1928 under the title *Lord Peter Views the Body*. "They are not all equally fine," says the Barzun/Taylor *catalogue raisonné*, "but so many are that it would be hard to find a rival entry in a competition for variety, balance, picturesqueness and sheer ability to handle detective ideas." I quote this to make it plain that I am picking on good work, not taking pot shots at any old Aunt Sally.

In the story called "The Footsteps That Ran," a woman has been stabbed and is on the kitchen floor of the flat above the one where Wimsey and his man Bunter are lunching with the local doctor. Bunter, before rushing upstairs with the others, hails a passing policeman, who joins them. The doctor examines the body and pronounces that death was instantaneous. Stabbed through the heart, but no sign of the weapon. What is the constable going to do?

Even a reader without any detailed knowledge of police

procedures must be roughly aware that a constable summoned to a murder has only got two jobs. One is to send for instructed assistance—CID, pathologist, photographers—the second is to see that no one moves the body or interferes with the scene of the killing until that assistance has arrived. (Chandler knew this very well. When a uniformed cop, arriving to find Marlowe with one of the not infrequent corpses that came his way, starts shouting questions at him, Marlowe says, "Don't work so hard on the case, son. You won't be on it more than ten minutes.")

Not so our passing policeman.

First he takes out his book and conducts a lengthy interrogation of the parties with a good deal of "Come come. Better let *me* ask the questions" and licking of his pencil as replies are recorded which seem to indicate that the murderer may have been an Italian waiter. At the end of it he says to Lord Peter, "By your leave, Sir. I'll be getting along. We'll 'ave 'im by the 'eels before long, Sir. Don't you worry." And when the doctor asks, "May we move the poor girl now?" he agrees at once and leaves the three amateurs in possession. Whereupon Lord Peter walks about the kitchen "turning over the various knives and kitchen utensils," and generally playing Old Harry with the scene of the crime.

But curiously enough none of this inaccuracy seems to invalidate the story. The policeman, for all his pencil-licking, is unimportant. He is, in theatrical terms, a walking-on part. The central character, the resolver of mysteries, is Lord Peter; and once the reader has accepted his role he can follow with pleasure the steps by which he unearths the missing murder weapon and puts his finger on the murderer.

My other example, *Clouds of Witness*, was Dorothy Sayers's second full-length detective novel. "It embodies," says her biographer, Janet Hitchman, "all those things which made critics furious." Among them she mentions snobbery and a painfully long lead-up to her clues.

But there is a worse fault than either of these.

Cyril Hare, himself a lawyer, put it in a nutshell when he said, "In this book, Dorothy cheats." He points out that the book is concerned with the prosecution of the Duke of Denver, Wimsey's brother, for murder. A promising conception. The narrative is, or should be, the building up of the case against the Duke by the Crown, along with parallel efforts by the Defense to defeat it: the basis of many crime stories both fictional and true.

Serious crimes, in England, are the province of the Director of Public Prosecutions. He is a barrister, with a small legal staff, and his duty, in a matter of such importance, would be to brief the Attorney General to conduct the case in Court. But neither of these functionaries is equipped to carry out the essential preliminary work of ferreting out the facts, interviewing witnesses, taking statements, and generally setting up the case which the Attorney General is going to present. This is the responsibility of the police officer in charge of the case.

And who is the police officer in charge? None other than Wimsey's old and close friend Detective Inspector Parker, about whom, at one point in the book, Wimsey is moved to comment to the Chief of Scotland Yard (another old friend), "Parker has been doing a lot of ungrateful routine work."

Certainly, but the work he has been doing is entirely directed to proving the Duke's innocence. His ambivalence reaches its climax at the trial, when a surprise witness is produced who is very helpful to the Defense. "It was Parker's diligence that had unearthed this witness, and he looked across with an undisguised grin at the discomforted Attorney General."

Certainly Dorothy cheated, and it diminishes the book. In what could have been a thrilling tug-of-war, the most important member of one team has not only been removed from his proper end of the rope but is actually found pulling on the other side. There is no burking such an inaccuracy. In this case the police work was fundamental to the plot. You cannot construct an inaccurate mainspring and hope that the watch will work.

These, then, are the simple precepts I would suggest. In a detective story, keep your eye on the ball. I am not suggesting that the author should cultivate dullness as a virtue. A properly constructed detective story can be every bit as entrancing as a thriller. To restore Dorothy Sayers her guerdon, *Strong Poison* is a superb example of the genre. There are agreeable frills, but no diversions from the strong central drive of the plot. And the police and the judiciary remain hostile until almost the finish. Perhaps Cyril Hare had had a word with her.

In a thriller, the plot, though important, is secondary. What counts is the atmosphere of the battle and the chase. Slap on the brightest colors in your palette; pull out the big stops in the organ. The sky's the limit, if you can get there. And only worry about detail if detail matters.

Will other writers heed these pronouncements? Most unlikely. Writers make up their own rules, which accounts for the infinite variety of their products.

Shut Up and Write

Donald Hamilton

Writers talk too much. At least beginning writers talk too much. I was a very chatty young fellow when I was starting out. Now, after fifty years of writing, I'm practically tongue-tied—well, as far as the subject of writing is concerned.

I've learned to keep my mouth shut about it because I've discovered that after thirty-odd novels I still know nothing about it; nothing, that is, that I can impart to somebody else by word of mouth. I suppose it's in my books and if you want my secret formula, look for it there. Don't come around asking me about it. I don't know what it is. I don't think any writer does.

What I'm trying to say is that young men and women starting out in the writing field seem to labor under the delusion that what they're striving for is a skill that can be taught, if they can just find the right expert to teach them. They think it's like swinging a golf club or shooting a trap shotgun or playing a musical instrument. Keep your head down when you swing or shoot, keep your head up at the typewriter, and you'll be another Jack Nicklaus or Rudy Etchen or Ernest Hemingway. Arch your wrists just so as you tackle the piano keyboard, or the word processor keyboard, and you, too, can be a Paderewski or Shakespeare or John D. MacDonald.

If only it were that easy! The fact is that no one can tell you how to put the right words onto the right places on the page to form a convincing scene or character; certainly no one can tell you how to do it with style and humor enough to hold the reader's attention. And no one can tell you how to take that scene and character, and other scenes and characters, and combine them into a reasonably convincing plot. It's your story, and you're going to have to work it out for yourself, God help you.

This is not to say that the experience of other writers is totally useless to you. There are several areas in which the budding genius can often be helped by the old pro. The marketing side of literature is one; the mechanical side is another; and then there's the simple question of morale.

With respect to marketing, I can't tell you how or where to sell your stuff these days. It's a very long time since I sold my first story. Everything has changed in New York, and not for the better as far as the beginning writer is concerned; so you'll have to look elsewhere for guidance. The mechanics of writing—the actual machinery employed—we'll get to presently. Which leaves the question of morale. It's very lonely out there in the wild land of the imagination. It's very easy to get depressed and start wondering if you've lost the trail completely; or if, perhaps, you're stuck with a phony treasure map and the cache of literary jewels for which you're searching doesn't even exist, at least not for you. Well, as I just indicated, this is a bleak country—the land of the learning writer—through which no one but you can guide you; but sometimes it helps to know that you are not entirely alone, that others have found their way across this wilderness before you....

I can't remember when I wrote my first story. I recall that, very young, I used to scare my even younger sisters (three of them) on stormy nights by making up appropriate horror tales to curl their hair. I must have been writing in high school because I remember clearly buying an instruction manual called something like *How to Type* or *Touch Typing Made Easy* and fighting my way through it with my parents' enormous old Underwood machine which gradually, somehow, became mine. I'd hardly have gone to the trouble just to produce some school term papers, although I used my new skill for that purpose, too. (At first the classroom stuff I turned in was practically illegible with X's and erasures, but the teachers didn't complain too loudly, since my handwriting was even worse.)

I wrote in college; in fact it took so much of my time that my studies suffered and I required an extra year to graduate. My degree was in chemistry; my father said this writing stuff was all very well, but I'd better learn something that would enable me to earn a living. He was perfectly right; and the chemistry supported me, and the family I soon acquired, for several years while I continued to beat on the typewriter in my spare time trying to learn how to write.

By this time, the ancient Underwood had been replaced by a Remington noiseless portable, a quiet little machine that probably holds the world record for unpublished manuscripts. I kept grinding the stuff out and sending it out with return postage. In those days, unsolicited manuscripts were treated politely if not always enthusiastically. I shoveled them out by the bushel, and not one of them came back stamped RETURNED UNOPENED, as I gather often happens nowadays; but in the end they all found their way home with little printed rejection slips. I was trying for the so-called pulp magazines, then in their heyday, but one day an inspiration struck me: what the hell, if I was going to collect rejection slips, I might as well collect high-class rejection slips.

So I took an oddball little love story I'd just finished—oddball because I'd never written that kind of a story before. I retyped it very carefully; after all, we were shooting for the Big Time now. I sent it out with the usual stamped return envelope. I told myself not to get my hopes up, and sure enough, some weeks later, there came my familiar envelope back in the mail. Okay. It had been an interesting idea, but I really hadn't expected it to work. I opened the envelope, just curious to see if *Collier's* rejection slips were noticeably classier looking than those of *Black Mask* or *Dime Western*. But what was inside the envelope, clipped to my MS, was not a rejection slip at all.

It was an honest-to-God letter from a real live lady editor. She wrote that my story as it stood was not quite suited to their needs (I'd heard that one before). But she went on: while *Collier's Magazine* had, of course, no intention of telling writers how or what to write, if I should be willing to revise my story in certain ways (specified) they would be happy to see it again—but of course they would understand if I felt that my artistic vision was complete as it stood, and preferred to leave the story unchanged and submit it elsewhere. However, in any case, they were eager to see my next.

Wow! I was in! Well, almost. I hurried to the portable and made the revisions as indicated (I thought) and shot the story back to the magazine with my fingers crossed. Pretty soon, back it came again; I hadn't quite got the idea, but if I'd try this way.... The patience of that editor was monumental. We rewrote that damned little love story together seven times by actual count, and I was beginning to lose hope; I didn't really seem to be catching on, no matter how hard I tried. But one day there arrived from *Collier's*, not the usual big manila envelope heralding the return of my latest revision of the story, but an ordinary letter-sized communication—although ordinary isn't exactly the word. When I ripped it open hastily, out fell a check for seven hundred and fifty dollars.

Along with the check was a letter from the magazine's editor-in-chief thanking me for my story and warning me in fatherly fashion against certain perils I might now encounter as a promising young writer; I should be particularly careful, if I chose to go with an agent, not to get involved with certain predatory types who battened on fledgling authors. I took the hint, consulted a brother-in-law in the publishing business, and got in touch with the agent he recommended, a very fine lady who did very well for me until she died some thirty years later.

Anyway, I was a writer, dammit. I sold another love story to *Collier's* and those were the only two love stories I have ever written and I have no idea where they came from. I sold a hardcover mystery novel that didn't do much, but then I sold a long suspense serial to *The Saturday Evening Post* and I was really on my way. The little Remington noiseless was retired to the closet where it still rests, a valued old friend and a reminder of those breathless early days. Its place was taken by a giant L.C. Smith office machine, which was replaced by another when it got shaky, although I think the name had been changed to Smith-Corona by that time. Electric typewriters appeared on the scene at reasonable prices, a boon to tired fingers, but not exactly durable in the early models. I switched over immediately, and I went through more Smith-Corona electric portables than my memory can keep track of....

But meanwhile. Back at the ranch. I mean, literally. You'd think that having got hold of a good thing, suspense serials, I'd stay with it; but Westerns had always been among my favorite reading and what the hell, if Zane Grey could do it, why couldn't I? So I sat down to do some heavy historical research—I already knew the country from camping and fishing through it as a boy—and I found that learning how those people really lived, dressed, and thought wasn't easy. First of all you had to dismiss from your mind everything you'd ever seen in the movies. (A real Western lady of the late 1800s, strolling down the main street of any real Western town in skintight jeans, current Western heroine fashion, would have been tarred and feathered and transported to the city limits on a rail as a menace to the morals of the community. A real Western lady wore voluminous skirts and petticoats down to yonder, and if you were that kind of sneaky creep you hoped, just hoped, that a wayward breeze would give you a brief, titillating glimpse of her ankles.)

Well, I finished that Western and sent it off with my fingers crossed, just like that early experimental love story. Again my gamble paid off. In fact I hit the jackpot. Not only did the novel sell as a magazine serial for a nice sum, but the movies took it. Naturally, I couldn't neglect this profitable vein of literature. On the other hand, I didn't want my name associated entirely with Westerns, so I started alternating them with suspense stories and doing just fine. If there were warning clouds on the horizon, I didn't see them, but suddenly the storm hit and *Collier's* and *The Saturday Evening Post* were swept away along with several other big glossy magazines that had seemed as permanent as the Rocky Mountains. With them vanished all my best markets.

However, my magazine serials were already being reprinted as paperback novels. Fortunately for me, the publishing house involved was trying something that was new at the time: a line of softcover first editions. The editor, one of the best I've known, was a man with whom I'd worked when he was at *Collier's*. He liked my stuff and continued to buy it, so I wasn't entirely homeless. The paperback pay at the time was, of course, nothing like that of the big defunct magazines; but it was money, and for some years I worked hard and, with my wife helping out by teaching in the local school system, managed to keep solvent by turning out Western and mystery paperback novels as fast as I could. But while we were scraping by, we certainly weren't getting rich or famous.

Then one day the phone rang. It was my editor in New

York, the same guy, telling me that my latest suspense effort was okay, in fact quite passable (he wasn't a gent given to superlatives), but there was a problem.

"You can't call the guy George, dammit!" he said. "Nobody wants to read about a George!"

I thought for a moment. Some names popped into my head from long-ago Sunday school lessons: Matthew, Mark, Luke, John. "How about Matthew?"

"Matthew? Matt? Matt Helm? Okay, that's not bad, we'll make the changes. Oh, and I have an idea. If you want to take a crack at using him again, maybe we can turn him into a series character, but you'd better get rid of his wife and kiddies...."

So Matt Helm was born. I'd created him in the first place as a one-novel hero because I was getting tired of writing about mild antiheroes who, after being kicked around for most of the book, finally pulled up their socks when cornered in the last chapter and managed to save themselves and the heroine. Apparently the nation's readers were also looking for a more positive literary protagonist. Matt Helm took off in a very satisfactory manner; he saw me through the next twenty-odd years in great style, and he is still doing well for me.

That's one writer's story. Now let's analyze the experience and see if it has anything to teach a young would-be author starting out today. Unfortunately the first lesson that emerges is that it doesn't hurt a bit to be lucky. I just happened to be the right beginner with the right stories at the right time; twenty years earlier or later I'd never have made it, at least not that way. I was writing rather polite boy-and-girl suspense and chase yarns at a time when the big glossy magazines were looking for just such material. I took a chance on Westerns and hit a wave of interest in those. I managed to come up with Matt Helm when a rougher type of character and story was becoming popular.

I could kid you that I studied the market carefully each

time I sat down to write a new story or decided to branch out in a new direction, but the fact is that I just wrote what I damn well felt like writing, and in each case it turned out that what I felt like writing was what some editor felt like buying. I had also, obviously, been loaded with luck in the first place to hit that incredibly patient lady at *Collier's* who helped me with my first published story, and I've been pretty fortunate with my editors since. So let's not blink at the fact that a hard-working, functional rabbit's foot helps.

But I will take credit for making a few correct moves. First of all, I was persistent. I kept on writing the stuff and shooting it out even when it kept bouncing back with yo-yolike regularity. Even after my first story was published there were times when the cupboard got pretty bare, but with firm support at home I managed to work my way through those tough patches. I know a young woman who consulted me about the MS of her first book, which I considered quite good, although I'm not an expert on the romance field. She sold it, and one more, but when I met her a year or so later, she said she'd given it up. She'd had to work too hard—writing at night and holding down a regular job in the daytime— and disrupt her life too completely for the few thousand bucks involved. It didn't look as if she were going to become another Danielle Steel very soon, so she was bowing out. Well, I knew exactly what she meant; I'd been there, too. The difference between us was simply that I couldn't really conceive of a life that didn't involve writing, while she could.

The next thing I did right, I believe, was letting the right person give me a hand when I needed one. There are two questions involved here. The first is: Who is the right person? The answer, as far as I'm concerned, is that the only person to whom you should listen, when it comes to revising your material, is the person who'll buy it if you get it right. This lets out all writing teachers, as well as relatives, friends, and famous authors passing through town. Their opinion of your deathless prose means absolutely nothing, because they've got no cash to pay for it and no presses to print it on. Forget them.

The same goes to a certain degree even for agents. You've got to satisfy an agent to some extent before he'll handle you, of course, and where business transactions are concerned his world is law, but don't take his literary opinions too seriously. One of my few unpublished stories (not counting that early flood of rejects) was written on the advice of the lady agent just mentioned. She had a specific editor in mind for it, but unfortunately he left the magazine in question before we could get it to him and nobody else ever liked it, including me. From then on we settled, in friendly fashion, on a clear division of labor: I wouldn't tell her how to sell the stuff and she wouldn't tell me how to write it.

But even assuming that you can find an interested editor to advise you, will you take his advice? This is question number two. There are writers who won't change a single one of their lovely, priceless words for anybody. I know one whose name you'd probably recognize who'd be much better known if he wasn't so stiff-necked about revising his stuff to comply with editorial requirements. There even seems to be a popular feeling to the effect that it's a bit shameful for a writer to alter his material on demand. What's the matter with me, mangling the perfect fruits of my genius just because some jerk behind a big desk tells me to? Ain't I got no pride, no literary integrity?

If you'll excuse the crude word, that's bullshit. I'm not writing as a hobby, to amuse myself; I'm writing to entertain the folks out there. If my story never reaches them, for whatever reason, it's a failure. If a little revision is the price I have to pay for getting the piece into print, so be it. But the fact is that very often a good editor can see the flaws in a story more clearly than the writer, who's too close to it. In many cases (hush, don't tell anybody) my final stories have been considerably improved by the cutting and revising suggested by an editor.

So I made the proper moves here. I didn't waste a lot of my early writing life soliciting advice from folks whose advice didn't matter, but when I was fortunate enough to attract the interest of someone whose help actually counted, I jumped at it. I have a hunch that my eager and cooperative attitude—the fact that I might just possibly develop into a useful author who'd be easy to work with—may have had something to do with that first sale. It really wasn't much of a story, and we never got it quite right, but it's possible that somebody in the *Collier's* hierarchy decided that they'd stretch a point and take it anyway, and get the poor guy off the hook so he could stop fiddling with this one lousy little yarn and write them something else, better. Which I did.

Another thing I managed to do right was mastering the basic mechanics of my craft and learning how to type with reasonable speed and accuracy quite early in my literary career—in fact, before my literary career had really begun. To be sure, Ernest Hemingway did pretty well with a pencil, but one can't help wondering if we wouldn't have had at least a few more great Hemingway novels if he'd started out by learning a speedier system of getting his thoughts down on paper. Nowadays, of course, the word processor is the thing, and I suspect that any aspiring author who doesn't buckle down and learn how to use one is handicapping himself seriously. The only trouble is, as far as my own work is concerned, that after a lifetime of working on paper, I can't transfer my affections to that lousy little screen. I have therefore settled for a big IBM memory typewriter hooked up to a disc drive that gives it an unlimited word-storage capability.

But the luck factor is always with us, from the brain cells we're handed at birth to the breaks we're given later in life. No matter what moves you make, you may not make it. I know a very nice young man with a very nice wife who, as far as I could see, did everything right. They lived on a boat in the marina where I keep my own sailboat. The wife worked in the local ship chandlery. For a long time I didn't even know what her husband was doing, although as unofficial author-in-residence I was often approached there by budding writers who hoped I could give them at least a glimpse of a corner of the magic formula for writing success.

Later, I became pretty well acquainted with this pleasant couple and he admitted that he was writing, but he never asked for advice or help; he just kept plugging away stubbornly. I knew he'd got as far as arousing the interest of an agent, not always easy to do these days, but apparently the big break never came in spite of his dedicated persistence. The last time I visited the marina, his boat was gone. I asked and was told that he'd given himself a certain number of years in which to make it, but his time had run out so he'd moved ashore and gone back to the kind of work he'd been doing before. Which brings up the important point my father made: writing is all very well, but when you're starting out it's advisable to have in reserve some other way of making a living. At the very least, as in my case, it can keep you going while you're learning your literary trade.

To balance this downbeat story, let me finish here with a tale of success. A few years ago I was asked to read, and comment on, the manuscript of a first novel by a young woman I didn't know. It's something I try to avoid for the simple reason that, as I indicated earlier, I'm convinced that there's nothing much I can do to help. However, I did read the story and send off a rather lengthy critique saying that it was basically a good yarn but certain things—specified— didn't add up, either logically or psychologically. Even though I hadn't been too diplomatic, I got a nice thank-you note; later I got a happy letter saying that the book had been accepted by a well-known publisher who hadn't agreed with my reservations at all, he'd thought it was just great without any changes whatever. The novel came out to considerable publicity and did quite well. Recently it got very good distribution in paperback.

Which makes me happy, not only for the lady's sake, but because it supports the point I've been making here: it's a big mistake for the beginning author to run around asking the advice of friends, relatives, teachers, and established writers. If that young lady had taken time out to revise her book according to my well-meant criticism, she'd certainly have delayed her success by months, and she might have loused up the story so badly that when she did get it to that editor he wouldn't have wanted it. The fact is that if you're really interested in becoming a writer, you've got no business wasting your time discussing your stories with stray characters like me. Or anybody else except an editor.

Just shut up and write.

Matters Grave and Gay

Joseph Hansen

In his wonderful essay "The Natural History of the American Writer," Malcolm Cowley says that in childhood many writers experience long, isolating illnesses. I was one of these. At the start of school, September, 1930, when I was seven, streptococcus invaded my small system. Years later, the discovery of penicillin would make strep infections trifling. But back then, medicine had no answers—certainly not medicine as practiced in small South Dakota railroad towns.

Doctors came, stood at the foot of my bed studying grisly charts of skeletons and of flayed human beings with all their veins, ducts, and organs exposed, murmured, frowned, shook their heads, and went away. To be replaced by new doctors who, in their turn, went away, never to come back. The truth was that either I would get well on my own or the virus would invade my spinal cord and kill me. Happily, no one told me this. All I knew was that I felt horrible.

But in the end it meant that since I was dangerously infectious I spent my days and nights, weeks, and finally something like eight long months, alone except for brief visits from my mother and father. Until I got sick, I had shared a room with my teen-aged brother. But now I had to myself my sister's pink bedroom. She was grown up, and had gone off to California to live, leaving behind a closet heaped with fancy, frivolous shoes.

I was too weak to get out of bed. So I lay, through a bleak, windy fall, an icy winter, a meager, tardy springtime, idly watching the northern prairie light come to the windows and go again, and listening to the mournful whistles of trains in the night. And learning to play alone inside my skull. A writer of fiction does this all his life, with toys increasingly hard to manage. I also read, but not a lot—I was too sick for that. I looked forward to the evenings when sometimes my father came and read to me.

But during one of my stronger and more restless times, my mother wondered what she could bring me to help me pass the time, and I asked for one of my brother's books. Not that I meant to read it. It was bound in bright orange cloth, and I liked the color. She brought it to humor me. I only meant to hold it and enjoy the look of it. Instead, I began to read. It was a hefty book, and certainly not written for small boys, but I read it all.

Later, I began to distrust this memory. Then, some time in the 1950s, a friend gave me a reprint of the book for Christmas, and I reread it. The experience was uncanny. Again and again, sentences, paragraphs, long passages jumped at me from the page, as word-for-word familiar as if I had read them only yesterday. The mind of a little child is a blank slate indeed. The book I had chalked upon mine during those long days in that lonely upstairs room was *Abraham Lincoln, the Prairie Years,* by Carl Sandburg. A writer-to-be might have made a hell of a lot worse choice. I was lucky that the covers of that old edition happened to be orange.

So Carl Sandburg became the first serious writer to put a stamp on me. The next would be Jack London, whose *White*

Fang I read and reread two years later during a Minneapolis winter that piled snow to the windowsills. London's *Call of the Wild* also stood among the Booth Tarkington, Gene Stratton Porter, Hamlin Garland books on my parents' modest shelves. I gave it a try, but its main characters were human beings, and for a reason I didn't then understand, I couldn't bear that. I wanted to read only about animals.

The Depression had snatched away my father's shoe store, our house, the car, everything. It had driven us from the only town, the only friends I had ever known. My father, a small man, was heaving coal into the mighty furnace of some gaunt, gray downtown cathedral. My brother was clambering around in the subzero cold, hanging banners on the Sears Roebuck building, coming home half frozen. And they felt lucky to have jobs, even though their paychecks were pitiful. We ate a lot of oatmeal. Somewhere inside, I expect I blamed human beings for what had happened to us.

It was one of those half-tone paintings that used to illustrate novels and magazine stories in the early decades of our century that lured me away from *White Fang* at last. This was the frontispiece of a book of my brother's, and it frightened and fascinated me. It showed a ferocious-looking bearded man in rags, climbing in at the window of a boy's room—the boy plainly scared out of his wits. I had to find out the reason for that picture. I began to read *Huckleberry Finn*. And when I reached the end, I started at the beginning again, God knows how many times.

So three good writers had marked me, Sandburg, London, Mark Twain, by the time I took up a stub of yellow pencil at the age of ten to write my first story in a five-cent Indian Head tablet at an oilcloth kitchen table in a bleak side-street apartment in my city of exile—though not, I fear, with cunning. I followed "A Hero of the Forest" with "A Hero of the Plains," and then, with adult praises ringing in my ears, retired from writing in favor of honking on a borrowed saxophone in the school band and learning to ice-skate. I was a bad saxophonist but a good skater, and as obsessive about it as I had been about *White Fang* the winter before.

But the Depression gave my parents no signs of letting up. They must have figured that if we were doomed to starve, at least we didn't have to freeze as well, and they sold what remained of the furniture, including my mother's cherished piano, to buy a stately old Marmon car with a bent frame, and head for southern California. As we all know, in southern California it is always summer. The only ice I could find to skate on was miles away, indoors, and accessible only if you had money for a ticket, which I did not. I went back to writing. And reading.

Bad as times were, hard as jobs were to find and keep, we always seemed able to afford one magazine, *The Saturday Evening Post*, and in its pages I found the means to while away the long lonely sunlit days of 1936 — the Tugboat Annie stories of Norman Reilly Raine, the cases of Arthur Train's crusty small-town lawyer Mr. Tutt, and the exploits of Mary Roberts Rinehart's eccentric maiden lady, Tish. If I remember rightly, these stories were often little mysteries, and it may be that they set my thirteen-year-old feet in their grubby tennis shoes on the path to writing that kind of fiction. Sentence for sentence, none of these writers was a Mark Twain, a Jack London, a Carl Sandburg, but they were first-rate journeymen, and their no-nonsense way with words I expect helped form my notions of how best to write.

It was two or three years later that Pocket Books came on the market at twenty-five cents a copy, a terrific boon to a kid who loved books and wanted to own some, but who earned only a couple of dollars a week delivering papers. I bought an anthology of English verse, *Five Tragedies of William Shakespeare*, and for no accountable reason a mystery novel, John Dickson Carr's *It Walks by Night*. It must have been the spooky title and the spookier cover art that made me waste that quarter. The book was all fustian and murk and absurd contrivance. I would use better sense next time. I moved on to Sherwood Anderson, James T. Farrell, John Dos Passos, and, when a high school teacher disparaged her, Gertrude Stein, who taught me in one astonishing morning the most important lesson in writing I ever learned—that every word contains a small explosive charge.

With such rackety schoolroom education as I was ever to get behind me, I set out to write novels that would make me as acclaimed as Sinclair Lewis, Ernest Hemingway, Thomas Wolfe. That I had begun to enjoy reading one now and then didn't mean I looked upon mysteries as more than time-wasters. Even after I had stumbled across James M. Cain's disturbing *The Postman Always Rings Twice*, it didn't occur to me that what Julian Symons would later style "sensational literature" could carry serious weight. For more futile years than I care to remember, I went on doggedly pounding out on a rickety portable typewriter gloomy novels no one wanted to print, supporting myself, my wife and baby with part-time jobs in bookstores.

Yet during those disheartening years, when it seemed always to be raining, I was learning my craft, not just by writing (the surest way) but also by reading as most writers finally learn to do, with an eye to how other writers turn the trick. And among these writers were such masters of the mystery as Erle Stanley Gardner and Dolores Hitchens, Arthur Upfield, Ed McBain, and a hundred others. They taught me how to write mystery novels without my even knowing I was learning. But not until I chanced on Dashiell Hammett, Raymond Chandler, Ross Macdonald did it occur to me that writing a mystery might, after all, be a fine thing to do. These men were real writers.

I made my first try in 1966. Two novels and a book of stories of mine had reached print by this time, under a pen name, from small West Coast publishers of doubtful virtue.

Publishers in the East seemed frightened of my matter-of-fact approach to homosexuality. And I wondered if, by fitting my chosen subject into murder-mystery form, I could get around these fears and reach a wider public. It came close to working, but after two years of near misses, I surrendered the book to a California porno publisher who insisted I interlard it with sex scenes, and it appeared in 1968 under the awful title *Known Homosexual*.

Watching the New York and Boston rejection letters pile up for that book, I wondered if the fault didn't lie in my choice of structure. It was a bracket novel. The murder takes place, the hero is arrested for it, and then we go back in time to show in order all that led up to the murder. This part occupies most of the wordage. To put it another way, the book is mostly novel, not mystery. The hero is not a detective, just a beleaguered black youngster trying to find out who killed his friend. I judged that since my subject matter was so touchy, I had better, next time, choose a strictly orthodox format.

I would write a novel in the tradition of Chandler, Hammett, Ross Macdonald, but it would be my book. I would hand the toughest, most masculine job in fiction to a homosexual. Because whatever most of us believe, homosexuals are not all hairdressers, interior decorators, ballet dancers. They work at all kinds of jobs, from carpentry to stock brokerage, from auto mechanic to college professor. In real life, private detectives were nothing like Lew Archer, and belonged largely to an earlier time. So I made Dave a death claims investigator for an insurance company.

This was a wry inside joke. Homosexuals well know how insurance companies feel about them. At least those homosexuals know who have been robbed and try to collect on a claim. Insurance companies also won't knowingly employ homosexuals. To get around this, I made Dave's father chairman of the board and managing director of Medallion.

Otherwise Dave could not have held his job for long. In *Fadeout* I wanted to tell a rattling good mystery yarn, but I also wanted to turn a few more common beliefs about homosexuals inside out and upside down, as many as I could in a space of fifty thousand words.

For example, people seem to want to believe that homosexuals are always on the prowl for young boys to seduce. In the real world, as homosexuals know, it is usually the young boys who do the seducing. The subplot in *Fadeout* of teen-aged Anselmo's infatuation with Dave is not the first such story in my work, nor the last. It crops up again in *The Man Everybody Was Afraid Of*. The situation is one of many hazards of day-to-day life special to homosexuals in our society. Its consequences can range from laughable to disastrous. I felt it urgent to tell this story to anyone who didn't already know it. And it crops up yet again in my mainstream novel, *Job's Year*.

The other wrongheaded concepts about homosexuality I dealt with in *Fadeout* have been pointed out in print elsewhere, and I won't repeat them here. One other point, however, requires repeating. Stereotypes were a hallmark of detective fiction, long and short, for decades. The pages of pulp magazines and two-dollar novels teemed with shiftless blacks, sneaky Orientals, treacherous redskins, conniving Jews, murderous Arabs—a long, shameful list no one seemed to think twice about, certainly not writers and editors. For the most part these have vanished—the stock characters and their creators. And a good thing, too.

But the homosexual remains fair game. From Dashiell Hammett's hideous little gunsel Wilmer in *The Maltese Falcon* to Joyce Porter's willowy murderer in *Dover One*, who stores his victims in the deep freeze, from Ross Macdonald's weak-willed middle-aged little theatre types in *The Drowning Pool* to Elmore Leonard's fat, sweaty, quivering Chucky in *Stick*, homosexuality serves mystery writers as shorthand for all that is repulsive in human form. By making Dave Brandstetter a decent, upright, caring kind of man, and following his work from book to book, I suppose I hoped I could change the hearts and minds not only of some readers but of some writers as well. I am beginning to wonder.

When it was finished, I felt *Fadeout* was the best writing I had ever done, but the manuscript went the rounds of publishers for two years before Joan Kahn, at Harper & Row, a small, stalwart woman in an office heaped to the ceiling with dog-eared manuscripts, somehow chose mine to read and didn't give a damn what anybody else might think of a homosexual detective, but sent me a contract for the book. It was brave of her, but readers turned out more hidebound than she'd estimated, and it would take many more books and many more years before Dave Brandstetter gained acceptance and his author woke up even moderately famous. After one false start, a decade would pass before *Fadeout* and its sequels found their way into paperback and the attention of a sizable readership.

The formal demands of the mystery suited me. There must always be a killing, a killer, a pursuer, witnesses, suspects, motives, means. The organizing factor in every traditional mystery plot is the same—the victim. The main characters always relate to the victim. A number of these characters must have had strong motives for killing him. The pursuer must uncover these when they are hidden, must sort lies from truth, and keep from being killed himself. With all of these requirements to fulfill, it would seem that the mystery writer has enough to do.

But I felt from the start that, as a hundred poets have shown the world fresh wonders within the strict confines of the sonnet, a writer worth his salt could freight a mystery novel with real problems of real people coping with a real world readers would recognize as their own. In a sense, my mysteries are journals that record day-to-day matters I see for myself, hear about from friends and strangers, read about in newspapers and magazines, or see on television newscasts.

The withdrawal of France from NATO in the 1960s brought into *Fadeout* that mysterious "man from France" who becomes the principal suspect. The victim in *Death Claims* had become addicted to morphine while in hospital recovering from severe burns—a problem medicine and society were not coping with at the time that book was written. I had seen its humiliating consequences in the life of one of my neighbors. The *Troublemaker* of that book's title is a crooked, down-homey lawyer preying on young women trying to collect child support payments from runaway husbands. In that same book, and a subsequent one, I touched on the tragedy of senile dementia as it overtakes Doug Sawyer's pet-shop-owning mother.

Los Angeles is a city that mingles races, religions, nationalities in colorful profusion. I have tried to mirror this in my books by including blacks, orientals, and latinos among my characters. Not only does fidelity to place and time demand this, but I love it. When I visit a city or country where all the faces are white, I grow uneasy. On the little side street where I live, the language spoken is Spanish. When I hear only English, I fret. But relations between the races here as anywhere sometimes fray. In *The Man Everybody Was Afraid Of*, it seems for a time at least that the bigoted police chief of a small California coastal town may have been killed by a black youth in love with the chief's daughter.

In *Skinflick* and *Backtrack* I deal with runaway teen-agers and the horrors that can befall them in the cities into which they wander and disappear. Related to this are the sexual mass murders that have occupied newspaper headlines so often in the past decade. I wanted to handle this, but it took me years to find a way. There was danger of trivializing something truly hideous by making it the subject of a mystery novel. At last I felt I had hit on the right method. In *Grave-*

digger, the shadow of the insane youth who murders and buries young women disciples in the desert hangs over the book from the very first page—but he does not appear in his grisly person until the very end. Even so, he proved too much for some readers.

In *Nightwork*, I tackled head-on the poisoning of our lakes, streams, underground water tables, our earth, the very air we breathe, through the heedless dumping of toxic and radioactive wastes by industry and government, a matter much written about, legislated against, discussed, but which no one is actually stopping. Instead, the problem swells, and grows graver every day. In this novel, to keep it honest, I did something I had not done before, and I don't know that any mystery writer has done—intentionally. While Dave Brandstetter solves the murder in the plot, he fails to stop the greater crime—the dumping of poisonous wastes by moonlighting gypsy truckers. To have enabled Dave to do this would have been to make him superhuman, a comic-book hero.

I never meant for him to be anything like that. This was one reason that I made his ongoing life story a factor in each of the novels. Too many detective heroes have no life apart from the case on which they're working. This is traditional but not credible. I was after realism in my work, and figured readers would identify with a protagonist who ages, loses friends, relatives, lovers to death and common alienation, meets new people, changes living quarters, quits his job to go to work for himself, begins to think about retiring, even at last is forced to buy a gun, much as he hates them. Letters from strangers tell me they enjoy my mystery plots, but the real reason they look forward to the next Brandstetter book is to learn more about Dave himself. Looked at from this angle, the series becomes one long novel about Dave Brandstetter.

While none of my mystery plots interconnect, and each

book can be read without knowledge of the others, sometimes characters involved in those plots carry over from one book to the next. Doug Sawyer, a murder suspect in *Fadeout*, becomes Dave's lover in *Death Claims*, the relationship continues rockily through *Troublemaker*, and breaks up in *The Man Everybody Was Afraid Of*. In the latter book, Dave has a passing sexual encounter with a young black TV newsman, Cecil Harris, who does not figure in *Skinflick*, but returns in *Gravedigger*, moves in with Dave, and, though badly shot up trying to help him (I received a number of get-well cards addressed to Cecil) remains steadfast in *Nightwork*.

Now and then, critics carp at me for making homosexuality a recurring element in my mystery plots, forgetting that ninety-nine percent of mystery plots involve heterosexuality, if not overtly, then tacitly. My handful of books weighed against those thousands of others surely stand no chance of tipping the scales, but fear and loathing leave no room for a sense of proportion, let alone a sense of justice. In fact, my books are not cyclopically obsessed with homosexuality but, as I have already pointed out, deal at the same time with a wide assortment of human perplexities, large and small. For example, struggles between parents and children crop up in almost every novel I write. But few commentators have made note of this.

My point in writing about such common human problems is not simply to lend my fictions verisimilitude, but to show that homosexuals live in the same workaday world as everyone else. In this way, I hope to dent the idea that homosexuals are all alike—the weepy damned souls of *The Boys in the Band*, the flamboyant drag queens of *La Cage Aux Folles*, the sexual hysterics who people the squalid night world of John Rechy's novels. In fact, few homosexuals are like this. Most lead quiet, commonplace lives, with their share of good times and bad. That all of them do not adapt gracefully to being odd man out I have tried repeatedly to show, because it is sad and true. Special pleading was never my aim. If Dave Brandstetter is an exemplary man, Darryl Cutler in *Steps Going Down* is not.

Whether I am writing a poem, a novel, or a mystery, the work is the same to me. It is the fitting of words together, the way Byzantine craftsmen fitted small bits of colored stone together to form mosaics. Stories to a writer of my kind are a given. So many come to me there never was a chance that I could write them all. Tidying up these ideas so that they make sense and carry emotional and philosophical conviction takes me an aggravating amount of work and time—weeks, months, even years. But this all goes for nothing if the writing is not good.

I get to the typewriter by ten-thirty or eleven o'clock every morning, weekends and holidays not excepted, and quit about three o'clock. Mental fatigue is quite as real a thing as physical fatigue, and working too long simply means mistakes of judgment will be made that I will have to waste the next day's writing time correcting. If I can get five hundred acceptable words (two typed pages) in four hours, I feel I have done a good day's work. If I am lucky enough to get a thousand words, I'm elated. I write and rewrite almost every page many times, in quest of a perfection I, of course, never quite manage.

What I hope I do manage is briskness, clarity, and surprise—surprise not arising simply from the events of the story but from the words and arrangements of words I use to tell the story. The best writing finds fresh ways of saying things without drawing the reader's attention away from the story to admire the writer's fancy footwork. Raymond Chandler ever afterward regretted all those similes and metaphors in *Farewell, My Lovely*. And I have had misgivings of my own about some of Alan Tarr's smart remarks in *Backtrack*. A little cleverness goes a long way. It is not a common commodity in life and so, in novels, can slacken the suspension of disbelief. These days, when in doubt, I opt for the simplest way of putting things, striving at the same time to sidestep the threadbare.

When reviewers notice my attention to craft, they commonly point to my dialogue, my "lifelike" characters, my descriptions. I give a lot of attention to scene-setting, landscape, weather, the sights, sounds, smells of places. It seems important in mysteries, where events can edge close to improbability, that they occur against backgrounds that seem real. If my characters are believable, it must be because I rarely explain them. A fictional character works best who is simply the sum of his actions. This is, after all, how we learn about strangers in life—a little at a time, by watching and listening.

Another fact of life figures in my approach to dialogue. Long ago, I noticed that most dialogues are in reality two monologues interrupting each other. Each speaker is intent on what he has to say, and half deaf to the other fellow. Since Joseph Conrad is a writer I esteem, it pleased me to find, a few years ago, that he had voiced this same idea, though in other words: "In writing fiction, it is rarely wise to let one's characters answer each other's questions." Dialogue that heeds this truth is likely to take two directions, which is useful to the mystery writer, one of whose handiest devices is giving the reader as often as possible two or more choices as to what to believe.

Like any other writer, I deal in all sorts of characters. I am a liberal in politics. But life has taught me to be skeptical of every system mankind has devised for organizing society. So much depends upon personal decency and honor, and these are uncommon. This may explain why I ended up writing about a man of decency and honor trying to right the wrongs people do one another out of greed and other unsavory, all-too-human motives. Other mystery writers rank themselves as conservatives. It doesn't much matter. An honest writer does his best to keep his prejudices out of his work. His job is to report. Judgment is up to the reader, once he has the facts. When I write about characters I don't like, I treat them as I would treat myself. When I write about characters I do like, I treat them as strangers I know too little about to admire.

Can the mystery novel survive only if it attempts to deal seriously with critical human and social problems while it unravels the tangled puzzle of who killed X? If I answer no, it is because human beings never lose their fascination with the myth of the triumph of good over evil, light over darkness, order over chaos. And retelling this myth is what every mystery writer does, no matter how he goes at it. My own belief is that the mystery novel, dealing as it does with that most solemn of events in any lifetime, death, ought to be sober in tone and treatment. But other writers disagree. To them, murder is a laughing matter. Still others like their murders cute and and cozy.

In the long run, I doubt that any single approach to the mystery will prevail. When my generation has typed its last pages, new writers will sit down at new word processing equipment and produce a welter of fresh whodunits. Some will be serious, some comedic, some arch. There will always be readers who crave mysteries, and writers to answer that craving. But most of what is written, printed, and read will be junk—as it is today. This is not exclusive to the mystery. It is true of all art in all centuries. Only the best survives, and not much of that. So, to return to the question—of yesterday's and today's mysteries, I believe those stand the best chance of survival that deal honestly and searchingly with the life the writer sees around him—always provided he writes well.

Popular culture is not as easy to define as snap judgment makes it out to be, but if we define it in terms of dollars earned, then universities are mistaken to list courses in the mystery under the umbrella of studies in popular culture. Mystery novels rarely reach the best-seller lists. In hard cover, not many sell more than five thousand copies. The most successful of the magazines that print mystery short stories, *Ellery Queen's,* reaches only 245,000 readers, some eighteen million copies behind the *Reader's Digest,* and not even on the *World Almanac's* list of America's hundred and thirty-five most popular magazines.

Who, then, does read mysteries? I know of no scientific surveys. But I do know that every now and then some mover and shaker in politics, business, the arts, or academe lets slip the news that he or she reads mysteries. The admission used to bring a blush to the cheeks of these notables. Even now, it is apt to be said with a nervous laugh. And this may explain why the mystery is shunted by some universities into a special category no one takes too seriously. Professors and instructors and administrators read mysteries, but still have a sneaky feeling that doing so is not quite respectable.

Since I have been asked, I think the mystery's proper place is in the mainstream of English department programs. If Raymond Chandler's work cannot stand up as literature against, say, that of Wright Morris, then let comparisons and judgments be made in a classroom where both receive fair and thorough treatment. To rule, before classes even begin, that Chandler may be taught only apart from other novelists of his time not only shortchanges Chandler but the student as well, a more serious offense. It may well be that some universities do include good mysteries in regular courses on the contemporary novel. I hope so. But even if they don't, I am pleased that the mystery has gained access to college campuses at last. Even flawed attention is better than neglect.

Or perhaps not. In a 1979 textbook, *Harvard Guide to Contemporary Writing,* edited by Daniel Hoffman, one essayist misidentifies the protagonists of at least two Dashiell Hammett novels, and lumps writers of wholly different talents,

Mickey Spillane and Ross Macdonald, as being of a kind. Scholarship in the detective novel has really only begun. The impetus of so many courses starting up may change that situation, I hope for the better. For some years now I have been teaching a course on the UCLA campus in writing the mystery. And other writers are trying their hand at this, here and there. My hope is that this too will help the mystery along to a lively future. The form has tremendous potential to widen and deepen our understanding of ourselves and our times, if only we take it seriously.

Mystery, Country Boys, and the Big Reservation

Tony Hillerman

Funny how you never rid yourself of the psychological baggage you collect as a child. At about nine, I became aware that two kinds of people make up the world. Them and us—the town boys and the country boys.

The town boys got their hair cut in barber shops, knew how to shoot pool, didn't carry their lunch in sacks, wore belt pants and low-cuts instead of overalls and work shoes, had spending money, knew about calling people on telephones, and were otherwise urbane and sophisticated. We were better rifle shots, better at riding horses, could endure hot hours feeding the hay bailer, and, until we tried it, were better at fistfighting. Thus the them-and-us division of my childhood was totally without racial-ethnic lines. Our Seminole and Pottawatomie Indian neighbors were part of Us, fellow barbarians teamed against Them, the town-boy Greeks. My Indian playmates, the Nonis and Harjos and Deloneys, were as sure as I was that the town kids looked down on them, not because they were Indians but because we were all country bumpkins.

I have since become old enough to know the above is mostly nonsense. Konawa, Oklahoma (home of the town boys), with its main street, two banks, drugstore, ice house, theater where a movie was shown every Saturday, and competitive pool halls, wasn't much more urbane than Sacred Heart, Oklahoma, the crossroads with a filling station and cotton gin, which was the center of our country-boy universe. But wisdom about such things doesn't change ingrained attitudes. When I met the Navajoes I now so often write about, I recognized kindred spirits. Country boys. More of us. Folks among whom I felt at ease. When I saw them standing around the fringes of a Zuni Shalako ceremonial, dressed in their "going-to-town" velvet and silver but still looking ill at ease, bashful, and very much impressed by the power of the town-boy neighbors, I saw myself, and my kinfolks, and my country friends. That begins explaining why I use a Navajo Tribal Policeman as my Sherlock Holmes, and The People who herd their sheep in the mountains and deserts of the Navajo Reservation as the background of my mystery novels. It is part of the reason I use the culture of The People as the turning point of my plots. But there's more to it than that.

The first Navajos I saw happened to be engaged in an Enemy Way, one of the curing ceremonials The People conduct to bring themselves back into harmony with their universe. It was July, 1945. I was just back from World War II, a very senior private first class with a patch over a damaged eye and a cane to help a gimpy leg. I had a sixty-day convalescent furlough and I found a job (in August, 1945, anyone alive could find a job) driving a truckload of pipe from Oklahoma City to an oil well drilling site north of Crownpoint on the Navajo "checkerboard" Reservation. Suddenly, a party of about twenty Navajo horsemen (and women) emerged from the piñons and crossed the dirt road in front of me. They were wearing ceremonial regalia and the man in front was carrying something tied to a coup stick. These were a far cry from the cotton-chopping, baseball-playing Pottawatomies and Seminoles from my past. I was fascinated. Forty years later, I am still fascinated.

What I had seen was the "stick carrier's" camp of an Enemyway ceremonial making its ritual delivery of the "scalp" to the camp of the patient. He turned out to be a just-returned serviceman like myself—who was being restored to beauty with his people and cured of the disharmony of exposure to foreign cultures. As it happened, it was the same phase of the same ceremony that I would use to make the plot hold together in my first mystery. But twenty years would pass before that would happen. (In fact, I called the book *Enemy Way*, but Harper & Row decided it would better be called *Blessing Way*, after another ceremonial that has nothing to do with the book. This sometimes caused folks to buy it as gifts for pious relatives.)

I wouldn't be writing about this interest in Navajos in relation to the mystery novel had not a lot of other circumstances coincided. First, I grew up in a pretelevison culture which was also often too poor to buy batteries to operate the radio. People sat on front porches, or on the benches which lined the front of my dad's general store, and told tales. A lot of value was attached to being good at it. In Sacred Heart, Oklahoma, being a storyteller was a good thing to be.

Second, Sacred Heart had no library. The nearest one was at the county seat, thirty-five miles away. If you loved stories, as I did, you ordered books from the mimeographed catalog of the state library, using a system which guaranteed a broad education. You would order *Captain Blood, Death on Horseback, Tom Swift and His Electric Runabout, Flying Aces,* and *Treasure Island.* A month later a package would arrive. Inside would be a mimeographed letter signed by the librarian:

> *I regret to inform you that the volumes you request are not on our shelves at this time. I have substituted titles which should meet your needs.*

These books would be *History of the Masonic Order in Oklahoma, Horticultural Chemistry, Modern Dairy Management,* a biography of William Jennings Bryan, and the Lord North translation of *Plutarch's Lives of Famous and Illustrious Men of Greece and Rome.* But now and then some chaff would be included amid the grain. When I was about twelve, the package included some of P. C. Wren's foreign legion blood and thunder (*Beau Geste,* I think it was) and a novel about a half-breed Australian aborigine policeman who could solve crimes in the desert Outback because he knew the country and understood the culture. The memory of this strange ethnology and a plot in which the grotesque, empty landscape was as important as any character lingered on. I forgot the name of the book and its author until, thirty years later, a book reviewer reminded me, accurately, that I must have been influenced by the late Arthur Upfield.

I have also been influenced by other suspense and mystery writers, the ones who demonstrated the rich possibilities of the form. (I suspect that half the other writers whom Robin Winks has enlisted in this project will be mentioning the same names.) Eric Ambler comes first, mostly because he never wrote the same book, or anything like the same book, twice. (For example, *A Coffin for Dimitrios, Passage of Arms, The Light of Day*—totally different, totally successful.) And then Raymond Chandler, at his best a better writer than Ambler, and a master of setting scenes which engage all the senses and linger in the mind. Not as versatile, but better at the sociological end of the game. Reading *The Little Sister* should make anyone aware that the mystery form, applied with craftsmanship and talent, can be literature. Naturally Graham Greene is on the list. How can anyone who wants to be a storyteller read *The Third Man* or *The Comedians* and not feel the urge to try the feat? True, Greene is an artist. But it's the master craftsman in him which builds the mood that makes the books.

I should mention others. The late Ross Macdonald taught every one of us that, given enough skill with metaphorical language, one plot is all you ever need for as many books as you want to write. George V. Higgins keeps pulling me back into *The Digger's Game* and *The Friends of Eddie Coyle*, reminding me how that Bruegels of Dialogue performs his art. And when I notice I'm slipping into those bad habits of adverbs, adjectives, complicated sentences, and turgid prose, I reread my dog-eared editions of E. B. White, or what Hemingway was writing when he was still young enough to care about it, or Joan Didion's superb journalism. When someone has emerged, as Didion had, as American grand master of non-fiction, the National Humanities Council or the MacArthur Foundation, or some such group involved with the betterment of our culture should bribe that person not to waste that talent on fiction.

However, I think I can understand what motivated Didion to take the step. Working with facts, as a journalist must, is like working with marble. Truth has its beauty but it doesn't bend. In the seventeen years I spent covering crime and violence, politics, and that "deviation from the normal" which journalism defines as news, the longing grew to take a vacation from the hard rock and move into the plastic of fiction. Instead of spending a laborious week digging out elusive facts, simply make them up. If you want a rumble of thunder outside the courtroom, then thunder rumbles. If you need a one-legged Navajo to make an ironic remark, you create the Navajo, strike off a leg, and he says exactly what you want him to say.

There's more to it than that. Along with the urge to free yourself from the strictures of fact and the onerous labor of digging data out of files and worming it out of reluctant bureaucrats, there's the headful of material every reporter collects. No job exposes a writer more often to that basic raw material of fiction—people under stress. It accumulates: the woman trying to recapture the logic that led her to kill her sleeping husband and her child, the teen-aged boy still smelling of smoke who might have saved his brothers from their burning home, but saved himself instead. The oil company executive who has just lost a bankruptcy battle and with it all he has lived for most of his life. The man on death row who believes his mother might claim his body and bury it in some private place, if you could only find her for him. The politician who has just lost his temper and shouted into the microphone a truth that he knows will ruin his career. The tense chess game played out in the legislative finance committee. The psychotic desperation of a prison riot. The hungry dream of the anthropology student hoping to prove a thesis in the dust of what was once a Folsom Man hunting camp. The teen-aged sisters in the sheriff's office signing the papers which accuse their father of raping them. All handled in five hundred words or less—or maybe a thousand if you have a loose edition.

Thus at the same time the yen builds to work in something more malleable than hard fact, an urge grows to try to deal with the meaning of all this. For me, it became specifically a desire to write *The Fly on the Wall*, which was going to be my version of the Great American Novel. Trouble was, I was having the problem all newspeople seem to have with that book in the bottom drawer. If you work with words all day at the office, it's tough to work with them at home. Each day you get older with nothing literary to show for it except a few more pages of false starts.

When all this was happening to me, I was thirty-eight. Marie and I had five children and had been living in Santa Fe, where I was editor of *The New Mexican*, for eleven years.

We decided it was time for a change. I resigned. We moved to Albuquerque. I enrolled as a graduate student in English at the University of New Mexico and lined up a part-time job as handyman, writer, caddy, doer of undignified political deeds, etc. for the university president.

The terrible moment had arrived. Naked and exposed. Nothing left to hide behind. No more excuses (or grocery money). Either you can write fiction or you can't.

My reasoning went something like this. While I intended, ultimately, to challenge Tolstoy, I wasn't ready to try *War and Peace, American Style.* That would run maybe 250,000 words, a lot for a fellow who has been conditioned to describe the Texas City disaster in a page and a half. First I would write something shorter, and something with a shape. I would practice on a mystery. I checked a few out of the library, took a look at techniques, counted words on lines, lines on pages, multiplied, and came out with about 80,000. That sounded like the Boston Marathon to a one-hundred-meter dash man, but not impossible. And, since I was uneasy about my ability to plot, but cocksure of my ability to describe, I would play out my tale against an exotic, interesting background, à la Ambler, Greene, et al.

Back to the Navajos. The interest rooted in the 1945 encounter had flourished. United Press had transferred me in 1952 from a job as state capitol reporter in Oklahoma City to manage the two-man Santa Fe bureau. Santa Fe is surrounded by Pueblo tribes, with their complex kachina religion and their secret kiva fraternities. Thus the Indians you get acquainted with there tend to be from the tightly built little pueblos of Santo Domingo, Santa Clara, San Juan, or San Ildefonso. In other words, town boys. Great people, but the country boys were for me. And the country boys were the Navajos, 150,000 of them scattered across their huge complex of reservations in Arizona, New Mexico, and Utah. I would try my hand at a mystery set on the "big" or central reservation. It would involve an anthropologist engaged in a study of Navajo witchcraft beliefs. His research would lead him into an area where my villain was assuring privacy for nefarious deeds by pretending to be a skinwalker to scare away the sheepherders.

Now comes the time to outline a plot. Right? Common sense seems to demand it in a mystery novel. I tried. A few chapters into the book it began sounding like nonsense. Tried again. No better. I decided to design a conclusion and outline from both ends toward the middle. It didn't work. Finally I put the outline aside. I would write a first chapter, perhaps even a second one, and grow the outline from that. I wrote a first page, rewrote it, rewrote it five more times. Wrote a second page, etc. Finally finished a first chapter. It was a fine, polished first chapter, made up of nicely honed paragraphs, good sounds, metaphors which fit, etc. I still have it somewhere in a manila folder labeled First Chapter. There are several such first chapters in that folder, each the product of weeks of work and each useless unless I can find a magazine willing to publish a series entitled "First Chapters Abandoned When Their Books Divorced Them." It took me several years to learn the First Chapter Law.

The First Chapter Law is, "Don't spend much time on it. You're going to have to rewrite it." It has proved true for me and I suspect it is true for all of us poor souls who can't draw a blueprint and have to let our stories grow as they go. (If you want to make that disability sound critically respectable, think of Minerva growing unplanned from the forehead of Zeus.)

I suspect I had the first inklings of this law about one hundred pages deep into the first book. By then the anthropologist who was the central character had taken on a distinct personality in my mind. (I can see him now, freckles and all.) He was not really the sort of fellow I had intended him to be, less heroic and more academic—the product of

134

the author associating with too many live anthropology professors, I suspect. Another character, an officer of the Navajo Tribal Police whom I had intended to be nothing more than a cardboard device for passing along information to the reader, had also taken on three dimensions and was clamoring for a bigger part. Add this to other factors and it was obvious that the wonderful first fourteen pages no longer led into the book I was writing. Out it went, with no more trauma than amputating one's thumb. I wrote a new first chapter which established mood, put the reader into the canyon country, and announced that the game would be Navajo witchcraft.

That short first book required almost three years of spare time, being interrupted by papers about Shakespeare, Chaucer, Milton, and Thurber, a graduate thesis, and the part-time job as presidential handyman. It was also frequently interrupted by moments of sanity. It would occur to me in these periods of lucid reality that no publisher would ever print the stuff I was writing, no one would ever read it, what I was doing was an unconscionable waste of typewriter ribbon. At such times I would put the book on the closet shelf to collect dust until the urge revived itself.

Even at that pace, if the book is short enough you finally finish it. In the case of what came to be *The Blessing Way* this didn't exactly happen. I almost finished it. All that was needed was a final chapter in which justice is done and all questions resolved in an ultimate flurry of exciting action. This eluded me. Finally, sick of the entire project, I tacked on an ending in which the bad guy is shot. I sent it off to my agent.

I had an agent because my master's thesis at the University of New Mexico was a series of experiments in descriptive prose aimed at a popular audience. The chairman of my thesis committee had recommended me to his agent, who had been peddling these efforts to various magazines. I had described my intended novel to said agent and she had advised me not to write it. If you have spent seventeen years learning to write nonfiction, she argued, why switch to fiction, which makes less money and is tougher to sell? My agent was giving me good, honest advice. The answer to that question, of course, isn't logical. It has something to do with the ego of the writer. You can't blame an agent for that.

I waited a month, then I called the agent. Any luck? No. The only editor she had shown it to didn't like it. Neither did the agent. Why not? Well, to be candid, because it was a bad book. It fell between the stools. Not a mystery novel. Not a mainstream novel. Showing it around would do no good for my reputation, nor for hers. What should I do? Come to my senses and go back to nonfiction. Failing that, rewrite it and get rid of all the Indian stuff. I'll think about it, I said. Send it back.

I thought about it. I had just read an article in one of the writer's magazines by Joan Kahn, then the deservedly famed mystery editor of Harper & Row, about the rich possibilities of the form. I wrote Ms. Kahn a two-sentence note. My agent and I disagree about whether I should rewrite a mystery. Would she be willing to read it and settle the argument? I got an immediate one-sentence reply. Send it in.

Those who have seen Joan Kahn's desk—or I should say the mountains of manuscripts under which one presumes there must be a desk—will have trouble believing the following. Only eleven days later I went to Amherst, Massachusetts, to visit my oldest daughter at the University of Massachusetts. On the way back through New York I called Ms. Kahn. Had she found time to read my book? Yes. Hadn't I received her letter? I told her I had been away from home. We want to publish it, she said, if you'll write a better last chapter.

At this stage of the game, I learned something new about writing. The MS was no longer merely a box full of typed-upon paper. It was an incipient BOOK. Everything was suddenly easier. Gone was the notion that this was wasted time, that I was only indulging myself. Someone out there was going to receive the message I was encoding. I found myself back in the familiar, comfortable world of the professional writer. I had in my hands a thousand-word analysis from a famous editor, full of shrewd questions and suggestions. I reread the MS carefully. The Navajo Tribal Policeman needed a bigger role to give the book its shape. I wrote a better last chapter (easy when the original is genuinely lousy), beefed up Lieutenant Joe Leaphorn's lines here and there, and inserted an entire new chapter involving only Leaphorn and a nameless horse. Finished! The next one should be easier. And in many ways it was.

For me, writing fiction requires intense, and exhausting, concentration. It's much easier to maintain that with some real hope of publication. *The Blessing Way* provided that confidence. It was a finalist for the Mystery Writers of America best first novel award, losing to *The Anderson Tapes*, a better book. Warner Brothers optioned film rights, Dell bought the paperback rights, and it was well reviewed. Trouble was, my scheme was to make the next book, *The Fly on the Wall*, more a novel of character than a tale of action. Unlike *The Blessing Way*, or any of the books I've finished since, I had a pretty fair grasp of the plot of this one before I started—or at least I thought I did. But when I got into it, I found my storytelling instincts at war with my urge to give the reader a truly realistic view of the professional life of a political reporter. If I stuck to the grand scheme I started with, the story was slowed. To keep the narrative moving, I had to cut out the details needed to give it that DEEPER MEANING that writers talk about after they anoint themselves with the sacred oil of art.

I will always have ambiguous feelings about *Fly*. It fell far short of what I intended. And, despite generally good re-

views, it didn't sell well. But it is still a favorite. I wrote it
from the single viewpoint of John Cotton, a introverted political reporter. I was totally comfortable in John Cotton's
mind, prowling a state capitol as familiar as the palm of my
hand and dealing with people I know as well as my own
family. I modeled the capitol after the domeless monstrosity
in Oklahoma City, but it might have been Jefferson City, or
Austin, or a dozen other places which used the same floor
plan. The highway contracting scam on which the plot turns
was something like one used in New Mexico (and, I understand, in Indiana, Florida, Oklahoma, and wherever politicians build highways). And the investigative techniques used
by Cotton are simply a description of techniques I had used
to dig through records (a technique made obsolete by com-
puter filing). Yet comfortable as I was with Cotton, even
before I finished that book I was yearning to get back to the
Navajo Reservation and back to Navajo Tribal Policeman Joe
Leaphorn.

I mean "get back to the Navajo Reservation" almost literally. I love the place—as big as all New England, a landscape of fantastic variety, a land, as someone said, "of room
enough, and time." I need only drive west from Shiprock
and into that great emptiness to feel my spirit lift. And
writing about it gives me the excuse to go.

For some reason which has never seemed sensible in fiction, I seem to need to sort of memorize the places on which
my plots take place. For *The Fly on the Wall*, I had driven
back to Oklahoma City and prowled the echoing old corridors
of the Statehouse to refresh the memories collected in my
reporting days. When I was writing *Blessing*, I climbed down
into Canyon de Chelly, puddled around on its quicksandy
bottom, and collected a headful of sensory impressions (the
way the wind sounds down there, the nature of echoes, the
smell of sage and wet sand, how the sky looks atop a tunnel
of stone, the booming of thunder bouncing from one cliff to

another). I seem to write in scenes, and to get the job done I need to remember the details of the stage settings—even though I may use only a few of them.

The way I put a book together, as a matter of fact, sounds on the surface like an argument for writing as a way of life. It provides a professional excuse for daydreaming—that most joyful of all pastimes.

While I always begin books without really knowing where they're going, I never begin a chapter without a detailed and exact vision of the place it will happen, the nature of the actors in the scene, the mood of the protagonist, the temperature, direction of the breeze, the aromas it carries, time of day, the way the light falls, the cloud formations. In other words, I need literally everything imaginable to be in place in my mind. Given that need, the question of "when do you write" becomes hard to answer. I write, at this stage of writing, while driving to the University in the morning. (So far, I have been able to talk the traffic policemen into giving me only warning tickets for rolling through the red lights that this kind of writing risks.) I write during those endless committee meetings which being a university professor entails. I write at cocktail parties, at the cost of sometimes nodding at the wrong time. I write in bed in that period of relaxation at the edge of sleep. Most of all, I do this creating of scenes while sprawled, apparently comatose, on an old sofa in our living room, or sitting on said sofa playing a solitaire game called Spider, which requires two decks but no imagination. Thus it is absolutely impossible to tell whether I am writing or loafing. My wife always gives me the benefit of the doubt.

It sometimes takes a long time to get the scene right by this process, but once it is there, correctly in place, the putting it on paper (more correctly, onto a word processor disc) is fast. The old reporter's conditioning comes to the fore. One simply describes what his imagination has created. Not much rewriting is required.

I do relatively little rewriting in the usual sense. My habit has always been not to leave a page until I have it the way I want it. The revision is done as I go along. I write a sentence, look at it, and usually decide it's okay. If it's not, I tinker. I delete the adverb (repeat one thousand times: using an adverb means you didn't find the right verb. Using an adjective means you need a different noun), reverse the clauses, get it out of the passive voice, fiddle around until it's right. If it's dialogue, I listen to it in my mind. Does it sound like this fat, short-winded, semiliterate fellow talking to a man for whom he has little respect? Right cadence? Suitably incoherent for the spoken word? And so forth. Takes time, but when I leave a page it's finished. There's one huge exception. I know from the outset that I'll come back to chapter one, and to other early chapters, to insert material and revise conversations. It's an unfortunate product of writing them without blueprints.

I begin with a thematic idea. For example, in *The Dark Wind* I wanted to expose Tribal Policeman Jim Chee to a crime motivated by revenge—a white value which has no counterpart in the Navajo culture and which seems strange indeed to a traditional member of the Dine'. In *The Dance Hall of the Dead*, I was interested in doing something with child-parent relationships. In *Listening Woman*, I hoped to take the Navajo mythology concerning the Hero Twins, and the dichotomy of human nature reflected in the myth, and play it out with a set of orphaned Navajo twins who have their own contrasting notions of heroism. As anyone who has read any of those books needs not be told, I tend to fall short of the original intention. But suspecting that I won't get it all done hasn't made my starting goals any less grandiose. Along with a theme, I invariably begin with a location or two—places on the Reservation where the action will take place, the Navajo Tribal Police substation from which my Sherlock Holmes will be working, etc. This gives me an excuse to go out and nose around, look things over, breathe the air, and talk to The People. This is an opportunity, too, to check the validity of any cultural details I intend to use. Has a tradition I intend to use survived in the part of the reservation I intend to write about? (A subplot in *The Ghost Way* involved Navajo avoidance of buildings in which persons have died. But would drunks avoid a favorite bar because of this? Anthropologists said yes. A Navajo policeman said no. I asked a schoolteacher at Round Rock. He had his class of Navajo teen-agers write a paper on the question. The verdict was unanimous. None of the kids would go into that bar. But those who drank had given up the Navajo Way and the teachings of the Holy People. The call of whisky would overpower the voice of the *yeis*. They would ignore the taboo. So, I had to replace the subplot.) I also usually begin with two or three characters in mind. One, of course, is the policeman-protagonist, Leaphorn if I want the older, more sophisticated fellow more comfortable with white ways, Chee if I need the younger, more traditional copy who is still curious about the dominant American culture. Oddly enough, others tend to be victims or secondary folks and not the villain. More than once, in fact, villains have changed identities in mid-book. In *Dance Hall of the Dead*, for example, the graduate-student anthropologist I had intended to be the murderer took on such indecisive, Hamlet-like qualities that I knew he wouldn't have the stomach for it. I changed the plot. Finally, I have in mind some aspect or other of the Navajo culture, and usually several, on which the story will be hung. These tend to be, indeed need to be, the sort of things which Leaphorn or Chee would know about and understand, but which would have no meaning to the Federal Bureau of Investigation, which has jurisdiction in my books— not because of any admiration I might have for the FBI, but because the FBI handles felonies committed on Indian reservations. (My attitude toward the FBI was learned from the working cops one comes to know as a police reporter, which ranged from disrespectful to contemptuous, and from my own observations of the agency during the J. Edgar Hoover days when attention seemed focused on keeping the vest properly buttoned and the hair properly combed. Since Hoover's time, the agency must surely be better than I remember it.)

The next step is to decide where, in the chronology of the story, the first chapter should begin. The first first chapter of *The Ghost Way* began in East Hollywood about thirty seconds before the victim-to-be became aware that he was marked for a killing. It proved to be exciting, full of tension, etc., but it joined my thick file of first chapters that didn't make it because it bent the book out of shape. The second first chapter began in the Chuska Mountains four days after the victim had been zapped. Wrong again. The ultimate first chapter, very short, opens at a laundry on the Reservation, about three minutes before the victim becomes a victim. I'm never sure how such intangibles are measured, but it seems to be right. It seems to me that the active part of the story should occupy as few days as possible. That requires flashbacks, or those conversations in which character A explains to character B what happened last autumn. I never mind reading those, and I don't mind writing them.

What I do mind is footnotes. It seems to me that I am writing what Graham Greene called "entertainments." My readers are buying a mystery, not a tome of anthropology. Therefore, my first priority must be to keep the story moving. The rule I force myself to follow is that any ethnographic material I work in must be germane to the plot. No fair digressing into marriage customs of the Dine', or the way the sexes were separated in the emergence myth, or the penalties for violating the incest taboo, unless it fits. I have no license to teach anthropology, having simply accumulated what I know through thirty-odd years of making friends, being curious, prowling around the various reservations, and reading what the anthropologists have written. In the second place, the name of the game is telling stories: no educational digressions allowed.

It's not a hard rule to follow. For example, in *Listening Woman* the motive for the murder of Hosteen Tso is to keep the old man from revealing the location of a cave being used by the bad fellows. It opens with Tso being interviewed by a Listener, one of that order of Navajo shaman who diagnoses the cause of an illness, determines what taboo violations have caused the patient to slip out of "hozro" into the disharmony of illness, and recommends which of the scores of curing ceremonials is needed. That done, a singer is called in to perform the proper ritual cure. Tso's responses to the shaman's questions lead the reader through a lot of information about the taboo and curing sickness. But they also provide the information which, while useless to the white folks in the FBI, is illuminating to my Navajo cop. To wit, late in the book I have Leaphorn sitting at the point where the canyon he has been following intersects with a larger canyon. His problem is to decide, in the gathering darkness, whether the place Old Man Tso got into trouble is up the big canyon, or down it. His problem is my problem. A toss-up. I could have him guess wrong and find something to identify his error. Or guess right. I don't like either solution, and neither would most readers. Here's a place for some Navajo logic, for which Leaphorn's Red Forehead clan is noted. I ponder. I go for a walk. What do I know about the Navajo culture that would tell him something useful? Changing Woman, Talking God, and the other *yei* supernaturals taught the first four Dine' clans the Navajo Way, gave them a thousand taboos, including bans against killing most of the forms of life which emerged with them from the final underworld. One of those was First Frog. Killing a frog induces crippling

143

illnesses. I skip back to that much-revised first chapter and insert the following:

> *"I forgot to tell you," Tso said. "On the same day the sand paintings got ruined, I killed a frog."*

I have the old man report that it happened when he dislodged a boulder, and include a few words of internal monologue on the part of the shaman illuminating the seriousness of this.

Now back to page 142, where Leaphorn has been sitting on his rock for about a week awaiting inspiration:

> *"From his left, from down the dark canyon, came a faint rhythm of sound. Frogs greeting the summer night."*

Since frogs are as rare as rich folks on the Navajo Reservation (where rainfall averages maybe eight inches a year), Leaphorn has heard a telltale sound. The reader has learned about the frog taboo, which may be useful to him someday if he plays Trivial Pursuit.

That same first chapter provides probably the best example I can think of when my writing friends try to save me from my slovenly ways and convert me to advance planning. I tried to plan that book. I had five chapters outlined before I bogged down in indecision. I decided I'd begin writing in the hope that this process would light my way deeper into the plot. I wrote the usual misfit first chapter, one of the best ones in my manila folder. Then I revised the outline and wrote a proper one which established the mood, the isolation of the Navajo Mountain canyon country, introduced the character of Listening Woman, and roughed in the dialogue which would be essential to the plot. I reread it. Neat, efficient, and dullsville. It lacked a hook—some interesting action. My outline called for Chapter Two to open a month later, after Hosteen Tso has been murdered. I could solve the dullness problem by having the killer show up in Chapter One and do the dastardly deed. But then he would either also kill Listening Woman, leaving no witness, or he wouldn't, leaving a witness who would tell the cops and convert my novel into a short story. I recalled that the mother of one of my Navajo friends had glaucoma. That disease and resulting blindness is a major Reservation health problem. Why not blind the shaman? Then how do I get her to this isolated hogan deep in the almost roadless country? Create a niece, an intern-shaman, a Tuba City high school girl who drives her auntie around. Kill off niece as well as patient while the shaman is in a quiet place doing her diagnostic trance. Then how do I get my stranded blind shaman back to Tuba City? I'll solve that problem later.

And so Chapter One is remodeled, bearing small resemblance to the outline. Same thing happens in Chapter Two. Introducing Joe Leaphorn alone in his patrol car in the early evening darkness proves too heavy on internal monologue. Insert handcuffed young thief/jail escapee into the front seat for conversation. Leaphorn stops the speeding vehicle of Gruesome George as outlined. As he approaches car to give ticket (as outlined) he glances at bad guy through the windshield and, since I'll need a label for this nameless villain, notices gold-rimmed glasses (as outlined). Here fatigue, whimsy, or inspiration interferes. Why not have Leaphorn see another set of eyes reflecting red from the police car emergency light? Why not, just to be different, put them in the back seat, causing Leaphorn (and the reader) to wonder why? So the eyes are written in, peering out of the back seat. If they aren't useful, eyes are easy to extract—especially on a word processor.

Next chapter. Well, why would someone be sitting in the back seat of this sedan? How about having Gruesome George hauling a dog? A big dog? A huge, trained attack dog? It gives me a way to add something to the villain's biography. It also offers other possibilities, since belief in "skinwalkers" who can change themselves from human to dog/wolf/werewolf is alive and well on the Reservation. Besides, in my earlier life as a reporter I did a feature once on training guard dogs and have a headful of otherwise useless information. And so, a dog (totally unoutlined and unintended) enters the cast of characters in *Listening Woman* and quickly becomes an ingredient essential to the plot. Later in the plot when I'm stuck for an angle, the rearrested thief also becomes useful again.

This business of having knowledge of how to train guard dogs and all sorts of other remembered material on instant recall behind the forehead has been continually useful. The Folsom Man dig site in *Dance Hall of the Dead* I first described as a profile article on a magazine assignment. The endless and self-delusive search for his mother conducted by the bent killer in *People of Darkness* was based upon a young man I interviewed the afternoon before he went to the gas chamber—willing to talk because of an obsessive desire to be buried in a family graveyard somewhere. The former magician, and the card trick so useful in *The Dark Wind*, goes back to an interview with a private detective. I wanted him to talk about detecting. He wanted to talk about his days with the carnival, making a living fooling people with "inertia of the mind." In the same book, the ancient Hopi survivor from the Fog Clan was based on a magazine interview with an ancient member of the Hopi One Horn Society. Again, in *Dark Wind*, recapturing the numbing ambience within a maximum security prison is easy enough if you've spent some time covering the riots, executions, and parole board meetings on the inside. Creating such stuff from go is possible, but it's tough if you are striving for reality.

And I am striving for exactly that. I augment my memory with a copy of that wonderfully accurate and detailed "Indian

Country" road map of the Automobile Club of Southern California. I cross-examine my Navajo friends and hang shamelessly around trading posts, police substations, rodeos, rug auctions, and sheep dippings. Good reviews delight me when I get them, but I am far more delighted by being voted the most popular author by the students of St. Catherine Indian school, and even more by middle-aged Navajos who tell me reading my mysteries revived their children's interest in the Navajo Way.

The best review I ever received was from a Navajo librarian with whom I was discussing the work of Indian novelists Leslie Silko (*Ceremony*), James Welch (*Winter in the Blood*), and Scott Momaday (*The House Made of Dawn*). "They are artists," I said. "I am a storyteller."

"Yes," she said. "We read them and their books are beautiful. We say, 'Yes, this is us. This is reality.' But it leaves us sad, with no hope. We read of Jim Chee, and Joe Leaphorn, and Old Man Tso and Margaret Cigaret, and the Tsossies and Begays and again we say, 'Yes, this is us. But now we win.' Like the stories our grandmother used to tell us, they make us feel good about being Navajos."

As a fellow country boy, I am proud of that.

Looking for a Programme

Reginald Hill

It is a prejudice academically encouraged that any crime writer achieving eminence does so by standing on piles of rubbish. Rubbish certainly abounds in the genre, if that's the label you want to stick on the unpretentious, the undemanding, and the unremarkable. A kinder metaphor would be to say that the crime-writing tail is undeniably long, but so I suspect would be the tail of the "serious novel" if market forces didn't dictate an earlier cut-off point. Different beasts cater to different tastes. The tail of the ox is edible; the tail of the ass isn't.

It's not, however, simply the pulp factor that confuses the critics; it's also the manifestly uneven quality of the genre's best shots. Chandler is arguably a fine serious novelist; Christie clearly isn't; but in the Pantheon, they stand on level plinths. The trouble stems in part from the fundamentalist approach adopted by most historians of the genre. They all set out looking for a common father, a universal Adam who started it all. Godwin's *Caleb Williams* wins the popular vote, though you could with equal justice hop back to Defoe's *Rox-*

ana or Nashe's *The Unfortunate Traveller*, or even *The Canter-
bury Tales* or *The Odyssey*, in the search for criminality made
literary for the reader's delectation. The truth is there is no
more a single starting point for modern crime fiction than
there is for modern society. Rather, in both cases, for they
are curiously interdependent, there is a gradual shift, with
the occasional sudden lurch, from one set of attitudes which
may be categorized as superstitious, aristocratic, and pastoral,
to another which may be categorized as scientific, bourgeois,
and urban. In the first condition, society's rules are essentially religious; man defects: God detects. In the second, the
rules are secular, and divine detection and retribution, though
perhaps still atavistically valued as fail-safes, are by themselves no longer enough. The significant new art form of
this evolving society is the novel; the significant new insti-
tution is the police force. The novel, being both radical and
popular, comes soon; the police force, being both reactionary
and unpopular, comes later, by which time prose fiction, having already undergone the same great spasm of experimen-
tation as the cinematograph was to experience in its infant
years, is ready to deal with it.

Put simply, there can be no detective fiction until there are
detectives. Once detectives exist, then naturally writers will
feel it necessary to invent them. The novel is basically a
realistic form and works on the material of the real world.
This means that the hunt for "the first crime novel" or "the
first detective story" is a hunt for an effect, not a cause; for
an antecedent, not an ancestor. Poe's handful of ratiocinative
stories are basically horror tales with explanations, like Mrs.
Radcliffe's gothic novels. It's the body up the chimney we
remember in *The Murders in the Rue Morgue*, not the process
of detection. This was certainly true in the case of an American student I once taught who, asked to expatiate on an
averred enthusiasm for Poe, confessed, "I can't say I've actually read many of his books, but, hell, I just love that guy's
movies!"

The point I am trying to make is that this generic approach, encouraged by the common-father hunt, can lead to a critical downgrading, particularly where there exists a predisposition to equate popularity with mediocrity. I had not intended to start off so defensively, but special prejudice has always required special pleading, and it seemed important to make it clear from the start that I think crime writing is worth close study, and not just from a literary sociologist's viewpoint. But I recognize that clearing the mind to make such study possible is not all that easy. I still recall with delight as a teen-ager making the earth-shaking discovery that many of the great "serious novelists," classical and modern, were as entertaining and interesting as the crime-writers I already loved. But it took another decade of maturation to reverse the equation and understand that many of the crime writers I had decided to grow out of were still as interesting and entertaining as the "serious novelists" I now revered.

It was this hard-won conclusion that finally released me creatively. At fifteen I had been ready to write a thriller. I even recall reading a book of advice on the art by, I think, Sydney Horler (does anybody still read Sydney Horler?). I don't think it helped me much, but in any case at fifteen there were plenty of other things to be doing. As for creativity, I wrote poetry, and continued to write it all through my twenties. It satisfied my creative needs while I mulled over themes for my great novels and powerful dramas. Not that poetry was an easy option, I should add. It always came hard. I haven't written much since I was thirty but now, approaching fifty, I find I can labor so long over short paragraphs of prose that I have hope that, deep inside, the young poet is still waiting to get out to be the solace of my age!

Anyway, there I was, thirty years behind me with nothing completed but a sheaf of first chapters in a locked drawer, and nothing published but a couple of short poems in *The Poetry Review*. As I look back, it seems to me that already my imagination was making irritated little signals, aided and abetted by the *Review*'s editor who, ignoring a whole stream of expressions of angst, weltschmerz, and other gothic conditions, purchased two poems which retrospectively chime like that warning tinkle of the telephone before a call comes through.

The first was called "Morning Ride" and features Death as a hit man. It begins:

> *This morning without metaphor*
> *death sat beside me on the bus*
> *and put his fingers round my throat*
> *with a cold professional touch*
> *asking if it hurt me much.*

I ignored the hint, but it was repeated even more strongly a couple of years later with the second poem. This was a piece entitled "Dénouement." It opens:

> *All in the library? Then I'll begin.*

And it takes the form of an interrogation of suspects in a "Golden Age" country-house killing.

At this point the telephone rang loud and clear. As I said earlier, the book I was working on assumed the dimensions of a thriller and eventually, much revised, became my second published novel, *Fell of Dark*.

It would be comforting to my self-esteem to say that the way ahead now seemed clear. Far from it. What had been released was simple energy and, like Leacock's Lord Ronald, I flung myself madly on my horse and galloped off in all directions. I had no programme. Creation seemed to me to require neither justification nor a goal. My first novel was published in 1970, the second and third appeared in 1971, the fourth, fifth, and sixth in 1972. By arithmetical progression I looked set to found my own Book of the Month

Club within a decade! But by the very nature of things, the heart must pause to breathe and the writing hand have rest, and I settled down to a steady annual average of two throughout the seventies. I tried my hand at many forms from science fiction to historical novels; I ran through three pseudonyms, and with this momentum was even able to ride the disappointment of a couple of rejections, even though one of them, a gentle satire on modern education called *Randy Brown's Schooldays*, remains among my favorite creations.

The major part of my output, however, appeared under my own name in the Collins Crime Club series. Here there was some control. My second completed but first published novel, *A Clubbable Woman*, introduced Andrew Dalziel and Peter Pascoe of the Mid-Yorkshire CID. I had no long-term plans for them when I started, but by the end of the book I found I was reluctant to drop them back in the toy box. Out they came again in *An Advancement of Learning*, and after that they have been regular in their attendance. But I was aware from the start that with the pleasure of recognition and the interest of long-term development, which are the advantages of series characters, come the dangers of overfamiliarity and stagnation. Therefore I resolved to entertain Dalziel and Pascoe only as long as they entertained me, and never to write successive books which featured them. These resolutions, at least, I have kept, and the solace of returning imaginatively to mid-Yorkshire after sojourns in foreign climes and distant times has been very great.

But this control apart, I reckon I was lucky enough to have an initial ten years in which I simply overwhelmed myself in fictions. Eventually there came a time to take stock. As a teacher of English Literature I had long been assuring often doubtful students that all artists had a programme even if they didn't know it, and it mattered not a jot that some of the writers they were studying might be baffled by some of the studies they were writing. My natural and professional bent was to examine and analyze what I was at. Also circumstances were pushing me toward a long-debated decision to make that move so deplored by Charles Lamb of putting myself wholly in the hands of the publishers.

One day, not long before I bade the joys of academic life farewell, a serious if rather dull colleague asked me in his dully serious way if I considered what I wrote to be "literature." I would have replied that I didn't understand the question, except that he would then have explained it, and possibly his explanation, too, at great length. So I said *yes* and moved away. I hadn't gone a pace, a pace—a pace but barely two—before I realized that I had given the only answer possible or necessary. And by *yes*, I meant that I might not put myself in the same league as Jane Austen, say, but I had no doubt at all that I was playing the same game. I speak metaphorically, of course. Once fiction becomes a "game" in any real sense, as it did in many of the pleochroic puzzles of the so-called Golden Age, then it bears only the same kind of relationship to literature that Monopoly bears to the London property market. I say this not to give offense. I love a good puzzle as much as the next man, and I try to give my readers one whenever possible. But I find it impossible to approach the refined complexity of the Great Puzzlers without losing contact with that still greater and more complicated puzzle of what makes men and women tick. A favorite among my early books (they are all favorites, of course! All flawed— I would do them better now—but all favorites!) *Ruling Passion* has as its epigraph these lines of Pope:

> *Search then the ruling passion; there, alone,*
> *The wild are constant, and the cunning known;*
> *The fool consistent, and the false sincere;*
> *Priests, princes, women, no dissemblers here.*
> *This clue once found unravels all the rest...*

Simplistic psychology this may be, but for me it describes clearly and elegantly that unbroken thread, spun by nature and nurture, which may twist and coil and snag, but, unremittingly tracked, will lead us, or rather the detective who represents us, to an understanding which is sometimes presented as a solution. The Great Puzzlers nearly always offer solutions only superficially dressed as understandings. This is comforting because it is noninvolving. We can say with Jane Austen, "How horrible it is to have so many people killed! And what a blessing that one cares for none of them!" But the pleasure I would hope to give (and the end of all my fictions is delight) has more to do with closeness than with distance, with recognition than escape. And, talking of pleasure, I like to laugh and make laugh because this is what makes British society bearable. The first thing revolutionaries of the right or of the left give up is their sense of humor. The second thing is other people's rights.

But the question remains, why turn to crime? And here I find myself returning to my earlier arguments against setting crime writing aside as a unified genre. On the contrary, it seems to me in many, though by no means all, of its manifestations to be in the mainstream. Crime is a central fact of human society; the potential for criminality is a central strand of human psychology. Our attitude to crime as expressed in our literature has always been ambivalent: part fascination, part revulsion; part outrage, part admiration. The criminal appears as hero as well as villain. And even the detective, when he finally puts in an appearance, shares in fiction that ambiguous role he enjoyed in fact. Dickens sings the praises of the new detective branch of the metropolitan police, then records with glee how one of them had his pocket picked on his way home after their interview. Vidocq, the first "great detective," a real character who fictionalized himself in his memoirs, rises, or falls, from being a condemned criminal to being *Chef de la Sûreté Française.* Mov-

ing forward, it's possible to see how the tensions of this ambivalence provide the creative energy for much of the best
crime writing. Poe's Chevalier Dupin is a strange, eccentric
creature of the night and, like his greater successor, the neu-
rotic, cynical, drug-addicted Holmes, a curious guardian indeed of the values of conventional society. Wilkie Collins in
The Moonstone wants his chief suspect to be both innocent and
guilty. Dorrington, in Arthur Morrison's lively stories, is a
private detective who outstrips the crooks in roguery as far
as he does the police in perspicacity. Conan Doyle's brother-
in-law, E. W. Hornung, brings the criminal-hero fully back to
life in the person of Raffles. And in the Golden Age even
the Poirots and the Wimseys are occasionally seen bending
the law in the interests of some "higher justice."

The best crime novels explore this area of ambivalence,
the worst merely exploit it. But explored or exploited, human criminality is so central to the way we live that a serious
interest in it is hardly a peripheral concern for the artist.
Whether crime writing is politically radical or conservative
in its main tendencies seems to me a question related to the
way an author understands his own potential criminality.
Those who see it as a fact of human nature will come down
on the side of authoritarian control; those who see it as a
product of social conditioning will plump for social reform.
(Of course, pushed to its absurd extreme, this suggests the
more conservative the crime writer, the bigger the crook. I
would hardly go along with that, though it could be argued
it applies very well in politics!) This opposition has been most
frequently expressed in terms of the difference between the
cozy artificial bourgeois world of much British crime writing
in the twenties and thirties, and the harsher, more realistic
approach of the American hard-boiled school. Chandler
stated the situation most baldly when he made his proud boast
about giving murder back to the people who committed it.
In defense of the "cozies" it should be said that he seems to

ignore the nature of the kind of British murder which requires a detective process to arrive at a solution. Over here, premeditation, whether of financial affairs or homicide (often the same), has traditionally been a middle-class characteristic. Things have changed a lot in the postwar decades, but in the prewar period, I would suggest that the fault of the "cozies" lay not in the social placing of their murders but in the psychological misplacing of their motives.

In any case, the confrontation in terms of Chandler versus Christie is clearly a mismatch, and more of a historical curiosity than a living reality. Differences do exist between the British and the American approach but they are certainly no longer analyzable, if they ever were, simply in terms of democracy and elitism, of artificiality and realism. The full range from puzzle game to serious novel is available on both shores, and it would be a perversely partisan publisher who denied the admissibility of a book on the grounds that it was too English or too American. But though our books are interchangeable, they are by no means confusable, and not just because of their backgrounds. Generalizations are generally dangerous, but only to the ingenuous mind that couldn't tell a detailed lie from a general truth anyway, so I'll go ahead and say that the main difference seems to me one of language and narrative style. An American describing an anthill will aim at conveying the whole seething mass; a British writer will pick on a couple of ants and follow them underground. The American uses language like a whip, to control confusion; the Britisher uses it like a magnifying glass, to bring up fine detail.

One of the delights of a shortish essay is not having to stay to justify yourself with cases, but some indication of where I find my own reading pleasures may, or may not, bolster my general assertion. Of the British, Nicolas Freeling leaps to mind. He has high narrative skills which latterly he has not been afraid to risk in his search for a more cerebrally explorative style. He also had the nerve and the sense to dump Van de Valk before he became a habit. Where Freeling is going is difficult to forecast, but I shall be close behind.

In many ways Freeling is now a European rather than a British writer, and I find that much of my greatest reading pleasure of recent years has come from the Continent. Simenon, of course; he does with natural ease what the rest of us strive after with great labor. Vladimir Volkoff's first two espionage novels have shown that it's possible to engage the reader at all levels in this area without the kind of over-writing that Le Carré sometimes wanders into. Umberto Eco's *The Name of the Rose* should for me have won every crime fiction prize available in every language it got translated into. If crime writing doesn't get possessive about the few un-doubted masterpieces that come its way, then it will indeed find it hard to complain when relegated to the lowest critical divisions.

Other British favorites who seem to find their best inspi-ration in foreign parts include old-hand H. R. F. Keating, whose Ghote books need no bush, and relative newcomer Michael Delahaye, who has moved from Italian art fraud to Israeli archaeological fraud, from small scale to large scale, with stylish ease. Of the British "big thriller" writers, I love the sense of seamless action I get from Craig Thomas, the steamy richness of Christopher Wood's Eastern settings, the Boy's Own pace of Ken Follett, and the engaging story lines of Desmond Bagley.

On the more immediate domestic front, I delight in S. T. Haymon's elegant wit, B. M. Gill's economic ingenuity, Julian Symons's stylish intelligence, and, getting down to our won-derful policeman, Jonathan Ross's flawed Superintendent Rogers and John Greenwood's rustically comic Inspector Mosley.

Across the Atlantic, I'm an enthusiast of Donald Westlake in all his manifestations, tough as well as comic. Gregory

McDonald's Fletch books amuse and intrigue, and John D. MacDonald's McGee books entertain even when they irritate. I wish I could be fonder of Ross Macdonald, but I have something of a blind spot here, much preferring Robert Parker as the postwar bearer of the private-eye flame. American police procedurals on the whole I like better than British ones. Ed McBain and Hillary Waugh are outstanding, the former for his control of the whole seething anthill, the latter for the ingenuity, credibility, and compassion of his police investigations, though I am not much taken with his later "gothics." Slighter, but still pleasant reading, are the stories of Elizabeth Linington in many manifestations. Joseph Wambaugh I admire but don't much enjoy. One of the best thrillers, in my view, to come out of America in recent times was *Tender Prey* by Patricia Roberts, who is an Englishwoman living in New York. Perhaps it was the combination of much of the best of both traditions that so recommended it to me. I find something of the same Old World/New World liaison (though to very different ends) in the delightful Charlie Salter books of Canadian author Eric Wright.

Finally, in this recitation of my personal preferences, the great heroes and, I would like to think, influences, of the past for me are, in Britain, Michael Innes (still, of course, very much alive and producing, but already surely a legendary figure), Francis Iles, and Conan Doyle—the last not just for his Sherlock Holmes stories but also for his historical romances in which he displayed those simple narrative skills shared by a whole host of British writers born in the second half of the nineteenth century, of which the most famous are Haggard, Kipling, and Stevenson. To tell a good tale is not the only writing talent I covet, but it seems to me to be the one without which all the others will be mere empty ornament.

I cannot feel that I have been influenced by Americans to the same degree, not as a young man anyway, but perhaps I should submit myself here to the great American shibboleth and say at once that I prefer Hammett to Chandler! The American way with a story, particularly a short story, I adore for its directness and economy without diminution of subtlety. Hemingway, Fitzgerald, O. Henry, Lardner, differing in most other respects, are united in this. And that great principle of the best American novels, *energy*, is, I hope, a contagious condition, for this is what I seek out most eagerly, and have found in works as far apart as *Huckleberry Finn* and *Catch-22*, *The Glass Key* and *Portnoy's Complaint*.

Now I've gone this far, I might as well drop in my classical selection. I love *Tristram Shandy* for its oddity, *Emma* for its heroine, *Pickwick Papers* for its labor-ward view of the birth pangs of a novel, *Vanity Fair* for Becky Sharp, who is a sort of Emma without advantages, most of Conrad, all of Wodehouse, Forster's short stories, and practically nothing of D. H. Lawrence.

To pass from influences to method, in composition I fall somewhere between Gray's fantastic foppery and Trollope's exact measure, but rather closer to the latter. I know there will be days when writing will be impossible, either physically or temperamentally, so on all other days, weekends and holidays included, I'm sitting at my desk by nine in the morning and there I stay till one, by which time I may have produced a couple of hundred or a couple of thousand words. Afternoons are for reading, research, deep thought, correspondence, plus the odd game of golf or the even odder bout of gardening.

I'm still very much a steam-age writer. I can't type. I've tried and the noise distracts me, and besides, those regular little letters don't reflect what's going on in my mind anything like the spidery wanderings of black or blue lines of ink. I use a nylon-tipped pen of a make which I'm not going to reveal unless they pay me! But I have used many a thousand of them and if I were ever the victim of an acid-bath murder and only the middle finger of my left hand remained, you could probably identify it by fitting one of these pens into the groove just above the top knuckle!

I generally start by reading through whatever I wrote the previous day, revising it in some small detail perhaps, and making marginal notes about any larger revision which I feel may be necessary. This is because I want to get on with the next bit and not finish the current session without any measurable progress in terms of length. Often I will have scribbled myself a note to remind me where I'm going next. Frequently these notes are totally illegible, and I have to press on without their help. Occasionally they are only half legible, and I am sure there have been times when I have inadvertently misled myself! I do, of course, have a broad idea of where a story is going, but there is a constant process of modification in the light of the opportunities that open up and the difficulties that become apparent as I write. Changes, of course, are nearly always retroactive as well as anticipatory. To change a character or a relationship in mid-book requires the whole build-up to be altered. Frequently what seemed like a very small thing in the beginning involves something like a complete rewrite. At other times, having decided to modify a character, say, I discover as I work backward that this is not, after all, a sudden decision but something I'd been nudging myself toward for a long time, and relatively little needs changing in the earlier pages. I have on occasion even changed the identity of the murderer, which might seem so large a shift of direction as to be artistically disastrous! But always it has been because the character first designated in my mind has evolved into someone who could not have done the killing, whereas someone else has emerged who could! Of course the physical possibilities then have to be built in by an alteration of details of time and place throughout the story, but these are the mere furniture of a crime novel. I don't think I've ever got them wrong yet, but I should much prefer to hear the complaint that my perpetrator was in the wrong place than that he was in the wrong personality!

Once a first draft is finished, I go through the whole book and do a detailed revision and reshaping, still in longhand. At this stage I find scissors and Sellotape come in very handy. Then the draft goes to the only person in the whole world who has a more than even chance of deciphering it, my wife. She types it out and passes it back with comments, often unrepeatable. I then go through the typescript, revising once more, and above all attempting to trim the excess fat. Characters, relationships, situations, backgrounds—I find that in order for me to get these right, I need to know far more than is necessary for the reader, and it's hard to keep this surplus out of an early draft. I should imagine that at this stage I cut between five and fifteen percent of a book. Now comes the final typing, the script goes off to my agent, and the three-pronged anxiety syndrome familiar to all authors begins to prick at the gut. First the agent has to get it, second he has to like it, third he has to sell it! The first a telephone call or an acknowledgment slip takes care of, but it's a strong source of anxiety nonetheless, and I am always careful to ensure nothing leaves my possession unless I retain a back-up copy. The second is not automatic, not if you've got a decent agent. On the other hand, he won't be too brutally dismissive, not if he's got any soul and any sense! He'll tell you you're a genius, *then* he'll say he doesn't like it! But if he's enthusiastic, then you know the battle's half won. There may still be another round of revision if an editor feels strongly, and persuasively, that something needs changing. But these are the pains of the long-distance runner who sees the tape in view and knows that no blister on earth is going to stop him getting there.

Curiously, revision is a process I've come to enjoy more as time has gone on. Ideally, I think now I should like to hold on to my scripts for a couple of decades and keep on tinkering from time to time till I get them right! But when I started, the thought of altering those immortal words was like Moses taking a hammer to the tablets he'd just ferried down the mountain. I remember my first publisher-requested revisions consisted on my part of removing several *and's* and substituting commas. Things have changed and I am now able to wield the surgeon's knife with a steady hand, not because I have less respect for what I have written, but because I have got more.

The other advancement of learning which took place was also, I suspect, common to most authors—the assimilation process by which the raw material of personal experience is tested against the needs of the story and not admitted until its color, texture, and taste match that of the imaginative creation. What must go is the self-indulgence of private jokes and personal references. Particular research into backgrounds is one thing; the use of what you already know is much more difficult. I went to Italy to get background for *Another Death in Venice* and again later for *Traitor's Blood* and a possible sequel. This process is one of observing, selecting, discarding, and is, in fact, much easier than writing a book set in milieus familiar from long usage. In *A Clubbable Woman* I used a rugby club based upon my own experience of the atmosphere and ethos of such a club. In *An Advancement of Learning* I used a north-of-England college not unlike the one I was then teaching in. In *Fell of Dark* I used the city I had been brought up in and the area of English countryside surrounding it. The dangers of close familiarity are not legal, though plenty of people claimed to recognize enough characters and situations to fuel a chamberful of lawsuits. (Interestingly, such identifications were nearly always wrong and, happily, few people are objective enough to spot themselves!) No, the real danger is artistic, that the familiar reality should become more important than the imagined story. We all know the type of tedious raconteur who grinds through acres of nonessential detail and would pause in his eyewitness account of the Crucifixion to inquire of himself, "It was on a Friday...was it a Friday?...no, it could've been Thursday ...no, I'm wrong again, Thursday we had that nasty shower ...it was definitely Friday!" To the writer, selectivity is all, and to the tyro, this is perhaps the most difficult process. Art should not simply hold a mirror up to life, particularly to the author's own life. That way you get stuck with one overfamiliar face and a lot of uncontrolled background detail, and in any case, it's all back to front. Most writers at some time are buttonholed by an acquaintance who claims to be privy to "the most marvelous story" which he would run up into a novel if he had five minutes to spare, but he hasn't, so he's willing to pass it on for a small consideration. Small consideration is usually what he deserves. Such stories are almost invariably only marvelous in the mind of the narrator, and the author has to be constantly on his guard against trying to palm such a one off on his unsuspecting readers.

I think that now after a couple of dozen books I am beginning to learn my trade, but whether I yet have a programme, I'm still not sure. The ultimate stage of reputation, of course, which comparatively few reach, would be to have a name so powerful in market terms that it would sell *anything*! Well, the money would be nice, but I don't know if I'm ready yet for the irresponsibility. Meanwhile, I still have to decide where I intend to go, with one eye closely fixed on the marketplace. I think I can allow myself the indulgence of an unsold script only once every five years, and I'm well up to quota at the moment. My intention then is to keep up my series of Dalziel and Pascoe novels, widening their scope now and then by a few degrees as I have tried to do in the later books, using the characters' familiarity not as a shortcut to a forecastable destination but as a starting-point for more complex journeys. Latterly outside Mid-Yorkshire CID I have experimented with a variety of thriller forms in books like *The Spy's*

Wife, Who Guards the Prince? and *Traitor's Blood*. In what sense, if any, these books can be fitted into a programme is hard for me to say. Certainly each has been a new test of my powers of invention and construction, but their biggest test yet has been in my next book, *No Man's Land*, set in France during the Great War. It would be difficult to include a mention of this in any conventional history of the crime-writing genre, but I know in what close relationship it stands to the ideas, interests, techniques, and aims of my other writing. It wouldn't exist without what has gone before, but I am in no way suggesting the process has been evolutionary, leading to a higher form of life! What I want to do is tell powerful stories powerfully. The traditional British crime story is essentially miniaturist; its patron saint should perhaps be Jane Austen. "Three or four families in a country village is the very thing to work on." It's a tradition I am delighted to work in and to try to modify. But there are wider stages, and if I fancy strutting around on them also, and can find enough people to be entertained by my strutting, then that's where I'll be found for some of the time, at least in the next few years.

That's *whither me?* answered in a kind of way. As for *whither crime writing?* I view the future with both hope and doubt. It is pleasing to observe, and indeed in a small way during my lecturing career to have contributed to, the faint beginnings of academic acceptance of crime literature as a topic worth serious study. But unless we are careful, the sociological centering of such studies, the concern with crime novels merely as a phenomenon of popular culture, may serve only to drive the genre deeper into a critical ghetto. I comfort myself with the thought that it doesn't really matter. History exists to separate the cream from the crud, and I am persuaded that when the literary pundits of the next century review the present one, there will be as many straight A's for crime writers as for any other group or pseudo-group.

Meanwhile, back in the dying decades of the twentieth century, with our political leaders seemingly determined to turn even the space between the stars into another maze of mean streets, the raw material of our craft is being pumped out in ever-growing streams. Here is one resource in no risk of depletion, and one day probably the last act of the last man will be some sort of crime.

Unless of course he's an author. In which case he'll be writing about it.

A Bright Grey

James McClure

Violence was part of my life from the beginning. That's what comes of being born at the start of a world war and having a professional soldier for a father. We lived at the South African military headquarters near Pretoria, and there were two antiaircraft guns right in our own backyard, between the lettuces and the tomato plants. The gunners, bored silly, would invite me to take rides on their guns, while they swept the skies for "Jap planes" that never showed up. I hadn't any idea what a "Jap" was until my grandmother exclaimed over a photograph that practically filled the front page of the newspaper one night: it showed an Australian POW, kneeling blindfolded in soft sand, about to be beheaded by a stocky man with a sword raised high. I can remember the fuss when it was discovered I'd seen this picture, too, and I can remember kneeling in my sandpit next day, making a mud pie, and being frozen by a sudden, sword-wielding shadow falling over me. It was my grandmother and her unopened parasol.

I'm still recovering, I guess; still filled with dread and fascination for the things men do to each other, and still making mud pies of one sort or another.

Then, after the family's move to Pietermaritzburg, the capital of the Province of Natal, our backyard became the focus of a different kind of violence. Real blood-and-guts violence: screaming in the night, the clatter my mother made snatching up bandages in the bathroom, my father seething, half-awake and revolver in hand. Often an unreasonable man, he was never worse than when shaken out of a deep sleep, and so as soon I could point the revolver without the muzzle wobbling too much, my mother would have me accompany her instead.

That began when I was about nine, I suppose. It wasn't half as frightening as waiting, hidden beneath the bedcovers, wondering if my parents were ever coming back. It was often almost funny. Like the night Miriam screamed, over and over, "Missus, *hurry*, missus! *Nicholas is killing me!*" And out we dashed, aghast, to find Miriam astride Nicholas's unconscious body, striking him—in time to her frantic cries—on the head with the side of an axe.

Miriam Makhatini, hired as our nanny on the eve of my sister's birth, generated more violence than all the other servants put together. She was a gentle-faced Zulu woman, her cheeks scarred by tribal markings; she could speak, write, and read English; she loved children; my mother took to her immediately and they became, without recognizing it until too late, closer than two sisters. "Poor Miriam," my mother said to me, when she judged I was old enough to understand, "she has a tragic life, I'm afraid. You know how Zulu men see women, as bearers of their children, and if they can't have them, then they're sort of outcasts. Miriam's barren, which is why all her boyfriends are such nasty people, wanting just to use her, not marry her, and that's how things go wrong— especially when they've been drinking." And Nicholas, a vicious-tempered member of the South African police, was a lot nastier than most.

I saw beatings, stabbings, scaldings, right there in our backyard. I saw Miriam married at last, after twenty-one years
with our family, and what a wedding it was. My mother spent
weeks making the long, lacy wedding gown, and my father
provided a sparklingly new limousine as the bridal car. I
drove Miriam and her husband, Richard Kosi, out to their
wedding party in the bush, stayed for a while, and drove
home. I heard next day that there had been a faction fight
at the wedding party, Miriam's new home and all her wedding
gifts had been burned, and Richard, beside himself, had been
taken to a lunatic asylum. He never came out, and Miriam
languished, dying of a growth in her uterus.

My other mother is still alive. My father isn't. He died in
1967, too soon to know how deeply he had influenced me
in what I'd eventually do for a living. Crime, as somehow
distinct from what went on in the backyard, engrossed him;
he read incessantly, everything from Ian Fleming to Homer
and two beloved, dog-eared volumes of Rabelais; and from
time to time, he wrote.

When sober, "the Major" (as most people knew him) produced the ponderous prose of his class and age; the style was
Blackwood's Magazine, Edwardian; the subject matter, his adventures in "Byzantium" as a military intelligence officer; the
allusions, largely classical, with plenty of the seven languages
he spoke thrown in; the paragraphs, enormous. But when
"gloriously sloshed," his meticulously-typed pages were extraordinary:

Small infant
with projecting milk teeth
messing about on carpets and mats and grass
prealablement avec petticoats
promoted to pants
  as pants the hart after the water-brooks
  so panteth my soul—or did, at any rate...

169

>   *dots is better than plots, isn't it?*
> *You utter ass, you were to speak of*
> *CHEE-HILD-HOOD, trailing clouds of glory*
> *and/or diapers*
>   *they call them nappies now, poor bloody idiots!*
> *Sunday books only on Sundays, a carefree if penurious life,*
> *soft rains, mild summers, good plain food from plain vans,*
> *plain speaking—do I make myself plain? NEVER on Sun-*
> *days.*
>   *Then the bottom knocked out of everything:*
> *"Did Cousin Campbell sleep the night, Nannie?"*
>   *(Campbell, a doctorly cousin rather than a cousinly doctor)*
> *"No, dear." "WHY?" "Because..."*
> *Relations fussing about and gossiping* aux *coins, God rot 'em;*
> *waiting*
>   *for the cortege to leave for the Necropolis, horrid name;*
> *marvellous repertoire of non-obscene epithet: blue-headed turkey,*
>   *monkey-faced kangaroo, ruffianly fellah;*
> *lovely high light baritone—"I wish I were where Helen lies, nicht*
>   *an' day for me she cries...." Daddy's dead.*

He made books part of my life from the beginning, too. They were in reach wherever I crawled, and could be dragged out easily to land with a satisfying thud. I built teetering piles of them, constructed tunnels of them, and, eventually, started to page through them, stopping at the pictures. Much later, I could read the captions, too: *Marat Stabbed in His Bath; Lord Lovat is Beheaded for Treason; British Dead at the Battle of Majuba Hill; Jack the Ripper's 2nd Victim....*

Even then, he went on reading aloud to me, so we could share *The Prisoner of Zenda, Swallows and Amazons, Coral Island, Moby Dick, The Adventures of Tom Sawyer, Great Expectations, Treasure Island, Two Years before the Mast, White Fang, Lorna Doone*—just some of the titles that come immediately to mind.

All rendered in the same deep, melodious Scots voice that, when my mother was teaching me nursery rhymes, had taught me to recite, "Lizzie Borden, with an axe...."

He sang, too. Sometimes it was "Frankie and Johnny"; sometimes, "I wish I were where Helen lies...." And told jokes, joke after joke; he was famous for them. Once, on an ocean voyage and for a bet, he told one after another from eight in the evening until eight the next morning, spending an hour on penguins alone. Our bookshelves were heavy with collected volumes of *Punch*, with P. G. Wodehouse, Stephen Leacock, Jerome K. Jerome, Mark Twain; our mealtimes, light with laughter—until I overstepped the mark by mentioning something as unseemly as, say, toenails, and then he'd boom: "You'll leave the table this instant, sir! God Almighty, there are *ladies* present!"

Banished with my plate, I'd take his chair in the drawing room and read, as I ate, whatever he'd left open when the dining room gong had sounded. It could be a library book—he borrowed at least twenty a week—or one of his old favorites, *Pantagruel*, *The Oxford Book of Quotations*, perhaps *The Newgate Calendar*, which was filled with particularly chilling woodcuts of splashy murders and had a musty breath. Then again, it could be his single indulgence, the current issue of *Esquire*, with its centerfold, cartoons, articles, and short stories all to be eagerly devoured, forkful by forkful. Ernest Hemingway, John Steinbeck, these were names I learned to recognize and search for, but I wasn't fussy—I read *everything*, including the text of plays like *The Night of the Iguana*, which the magazine ran in full on buff-colored pages. This, I'm pretty sure, was my education.

Because, so far as ordinary schooling went, I did very poorly in most subjects and so badly in Afrikaans that I left without graduating, unable to go to unversity. My father had something to do with this, too. He'd always dismissed Afrikaans as "that damned Dutch patois," even refusing to help me with my Afrikaans spelling homework, although I argued his facility with German should have made it possible for him to pronounce the words I needed to be tested on. Then, during the last night we ever spent together, we went to his club and there I heard him speaking fluent, jovially colloquial Afrikaans to a senator. My father, I learned, had taught himself the language on the three-week voyage that brought him out to South Africa long, long before I was born.

Esquire had an obvious effect during my last years at high school. I became notorious for short stories that turned the stomachs of the less robust English teachers. In *Pride and Joy?* Mrs. Feldstein calls on Mrs. Bishopstowe, and while they're having tea on the patio, little Manny and Penny go up to the playroom. "My Manny," says Mrs. Feldstein, "has such an interest in medicine, you know—such *sensitive* hands. A surgeon, he wants to be already, and he's not even turned six!" "Well, my Penny's not five yet, darling," says Mrs. Bishopstowe, "and so *terribly* gifted. Her drama teacher is quite overwhelmed, she says, by such a *range of expression* in one so young. Just imagine, a *star* in the family!" The scene cuts to Manny talking Penny into playing "doctors and nurses," and then back to the mothers, now really wallowing in parental pride. This cross-cutting continues, with Penny acting the part of a patient, and the mothers, who can hear snatches of the "realistic" conversation from the window above, waxing excessively smug, until Penny starts screaming rather too loudly and the children are called down. There is a sudden silence, then Manny comes out on to the patio alone, smiling cutely and carrying a small foot.

Dr. John Clarke, who marked this, wrote and sold some pretty macabre short stories himself, so he reacted with constructive criticism and with encouragement, rather than with the usual, "Yeeergh!" Even so, I don't think I thought for one moment of ever becoming a writer. I already had an identity that suited me fine.

For years and years, people had been saying, "Gosh, you're an artist...." What they meant was, I could draw and paint reasonably well, and had used these skills—learned by example from both my parents—to win a succession of prizes for my school.

And then, when I grew dissatisfied with "art" as a medium of expression, mainly because I just couldn't paint well enough to convey what I wanted to, I switched to using a camera, won more prizes, and decided I was in fact a photographer. This suited me even better for a while, since at last I was able to document accurately the fascinating, often grotesque world around me. Much influenced by the great *Life* photojournalists, Robert Capa, et al., I'd spend almost every weekend exploring black shanty towns, going to Hindu funerals and weddings, compiling "photo essays" on topics as various as Zulu boxers and the "poor whites" and their tattooed children, who lived up beyond the station.

Photography was my living for almost a year. I worked for a local commercial studio, starting the day I left school by taking the class graduation picture, and later joined Tom Sharpe, who had just set up his own studio in town. We had been good friends for some time, but one night his life style finally proved too much for me—it's a long story, involving an orangutan and a political activist with a flick knife—so I quit.

A week later, I saw Danny Kaye in a film about a boys' preparatory school, and wrote to my old headmaster, asking if I could make myself useful. For the next four and a bit years, I taught English, art, and history, and spent my holidays exploring remote areas in my jeep. I also did some writing, chiefly because it seemed expedient to do so. The twice-a-year school plays were my responsibility, and when I was unable to find something suitable for a particular age group, I composed something myself, subject to the headmaster's approval. *Father to the Mushroom* revolved around the discovery of fire, with the "cavemen" reacting with the same mixed feelings their descendants would have for atomic energy. *Coolahah*, a rousing tale of American pioneers, Red Indians, and a foolhardy missionary, proved the greatest hit and gave the school its first "extended run," not least because of a "realism" that became fractionally excessive on the last night. That was when several of the two dozen .38 "blanks" fired over the outdoor audience from behind, during an attack on the pioneers' fort, richocheted *live* off the tin roof of a neighboring farmhouse; and when the missionary took an arrow in the gut, he vomited his mouthful of tomato ketchup "blood" right into a hot footlight, causing one hell of a bang and fusing all the lights.

But I still didn't think of myself as a writer. Not even after I turned a long tale, improvised for the benefit of the senior dormitory, into *Maputoland Adventure*, a 40,000-word teen-age novel that my father typed out for me. The manuscript was twice almost accepted, subject to revisions, and then I forgot about it. Neither did I think of myself as a poet, although some of my work had been published in the University of Natal students' newspaper, and the English Department had invited me to give a reading. I was simply too taken up with my new identity as a journalist.

This, the undoubted turning point in my life, came about as haphazardly as most things in those days. I went out one midnight to buy some Lucky Strikes, and bumped into some-one I hadn't seen for years. "And how are you doing?" he asked. "Oh, not so great," I replied. "I'm married now and we can't really get by on an unqualified teacher's salary." "Then why not apply for my job?" he suggested. "Subeditor on the *Natal Witness*—I've just resigned." I wrote and got the job—all without daring to ask, in case I'd feel intimidated, exactly what a subeditor *did*.

I discovered soon enough: we cut stories to length, corrected spelling, revised sloppy writing, thought up headlines, and schemed pages. I loved it. Not only the undeniable gratification of seeing one's work in print, and *so soon after* one had written it, but all the other old clichés as well: the smell of the ink, the excitement of being right there when a big story broke. I can remember moving aside my coffee mug on a Telex machine one night, glancing at the roll of paper below, and reading a "flash" that President Kennedy had been shot.

Then I started photography again. At first, I made picture features in my spare time. But after a while, when late-night accidents and disasters struck, I would be sent to cover them from the subeditors' table, as this was often quicker than alerting the duty photographer. This brought me for the first time into regular contact with the South African police, and a fascination began to grow, based on so many paradoxes. There was the time, for instance, when I was asked to open the refrigerator in the police mortuary, as the officers I was with had their hands very full. To my astonishment, in a land where the very park benches carried signs saying whether they were "black" or "white," the doors swung back to reveal black corpses *and* white corpses all crowded in together, higgledy-piggledy, without a hint of segregation.

As soon as possible, I had quit the subeditors' room to work as a reporter cum photographer. Politics, poltergeists, "human interest" stories, and record trout catches were a large part of my brief. But mainly I covered both magistrates' hearings and the Supreme Court, did police calls, hospital calls, and almost set up home at the fire station, which also provided the city's ambulance service. I became obsessed, working sixteen hours most days, and later, when I joined the *Natal Mercury*, I went thirteen months without taking a holiday or a full weekend. I had to see it *all*, I guess.

I saw too much. In 1965, my American wife, Lorly, our first-born, James, and I landed at Turnhouse Airport near Edinburgh. We had two suitcases and less than enough money to last a month, but I was again lucky, landing a subeditor's job with the *Daily Mail* on the sixth day. I was hired by a Scot who had spent several happy months convalescing in Pietermaritzburg during World War Two, and wanted to ask nostalgic questions about it.

Our first home in Britain had no backyard. It was a basement, an almost windowless hole in the ground, and that is where the dreams began. Long, orderly documentaries that were utterly undreamlike, but examples of a form of total recall so complete that my right thigh would remember to swing out of the way of a historic chest that stood in a narrow corridor at the magistrates' courts. Day after day returned to me, some uneventful and quite ordinary, others horrifying. Often I'd wake sweating, fearful of falling asleep again. Now, I saw even more than I had done before, feeling free to pause and reflect.

But I had nothing actually before me to see and paint, to capture with a camera. This was the reason, I think, I began to type, to really want to write for the first time in my life. I started with short stories, none of which in fact touched on the immediate past, but were drawn from my schoolteacher days. They were all stillbirths.

It never occurred to me to try a book.

Some four years later, Lorly, me, James, and two additions to the family, Alistair and Kirsten, were living in a tiny flat in Oxford so cramped that nobody slept as much as an arm's length from anyone else. We had moved south hoping to save for the deposit on a house, but each month saw my pay, as a subeditor on the *Oxford Mail*, swallowed up by sheer necessities. Although we did have one extravagance, a hired television set.

Television was still the novelty for us it had been when we'd seen it for the first time ever on our arrival in Scotland.

I watched pretty well everything, as we could never afford to go out, and soon developed a particular enthusiasm for BBC drama, which nonetheless had its disappointments. One night I said, "Hell, I could've written a play at least as good as that!" And sat down at my typewriter as soon as the last program was over, wondering what to write about. That last program had been a documentary on the war in Vietnam, so I began *The Hole*, using as my opening shot the last shot I'd just seen.

The play was finished in a matter of days. It told the story of an American GI who becomes trapped in a Vietcong tunnel during a search-and-destroy mission, and then finds he is entombed with a Vietnamese couple and their baby. The story had many levels, but I made sure that one of them would engross, I hoped, the tired dock worker with a bottle of beer in one hand and an interest in only "How the Jesus is that poor bastard going to get out?" Escapism for escapists, I suppose one could call it, with more if one wanted more.

For a brief period, events moved with fairy-tale swiftness and simplicity. An agency snapped up *The Hole* and showed it to Tony Garnett, the BBC *wunderkind* of the time. He invited me to dinner, and told me he wanted to make it. This was magic, promising instant fame overnight, and what was more, there was no talk of an extensive rewrite. The story line, dialogue, and structure—which, I realize now, owed so much to those years of *Esquire*—won only praise from him. But, as I took Cloud Nine back to Oxford, I was about to be hoist with my own petard.

In planning *The Hole*, I had kept everything to the bare minimum—two clips of stock film, one set, only one real speaking part, four actors—in the hope of attracting a sale because it promised to be very cheap to make. Tony Garnett, however, decided that so much depended on getting the right "reaction shots" from the virtually silent Vietnamese, he'd want to shoot on film as opposed to making a "live" video recording. This called for a relatively enormous budget, and when there was an actors' union protest over how few players were involved in what had become a major production, *The Hole* was handed back to me.

A lot of time had gone by; our flat had become even smaller as the children had grown larger. I was getting quite desperate when suddenly Granada Television, the commercial channel's answer to the BBC, bought the play for enough for a house deposit. Scriptwriting, I thought, was the answer to everything.

So we moved into our new home, and I wrote *Roll Me A Snowball*, in which CBS took a passing interest. I heard that *The Hole* was about to go into rehearsal with John Shrapnel of the Royal Shakespeare Company in the lead, and much encouraged, wrote *Coach to Valhalla*. It didn't leave the depot. I read in the papers that there was a television directors' strike, and shortly afterward learned that *The Hole*, along with seven other plays earmarked for a drama season, had been abandoned. I thought of naming our house, in discreetly ironic pokerwork on a slice of beech, Granada's Folly.

I stopped writing. *The Hole* was taken up by a film production company, many nice things were said, many meetings were held, script changes were ordered, everyone wanted to leave his or her mark on it, the producer went to Italy to find the money. He must have found something else, because he didn't return—or if he did, nobody told me. I felt even less like writing.

I switched to the *Oxford Times*, threw myself into building up a features department, and took to cartooning.

Then one lunchtime, when Anthony Prince, the chief subeditor, and I went out for our customary stroll and a pint, he dropped into the post office to mail a parcel. He told me it was the manuscript of his first novel, *The Labyrinth Makers*, and we drank to its success. Ten days later, a contract arrived from Gollancz—and the book went on to win the Silver Dagger, presented by the Crime Writers' Association.

My God, I thought, this is *very* different from television. It's like being a chair maker; if you offer a chair, and people like sitting in it, that's that: they buy the damn thing.

Not long after that, I had two weeks' vacation and no money for a holiday away. The house was bleak for want of furniture, and the garage stood empty. On the first night of that vacation, I dragged out my typewriter and sat down to write a novel, hoping this would change things.

I'd no idea of what sort of book it would be, nor how to begin it. So I cast around for a first sentence, *any* sentence. The previous Saturday, while earning extra money by subediting the *Oxford Mail's* football special, I'd done some doodling, waiting for the half-time scores. Practicing Gothic lettering, I had printed: "For an undertaker, George Henry Abbott was a sad man." I don't know why. But as this was the only sentence I had at hand, I typed it—and the rest of the chapter followed, as though I were witnessing it unfold.

Then, having established that foul play had been committed, it was only natural to introduce a detective in Chapter Two. Again, I just saw and heard the man, and learned his name was Kramer. I hurried on, pausing only to decide where the murder had taken place. For fun and with mild malice, I imagined it being in Tom Sharpe's cottage at the rear of a property where Lorly and I had first set up home. Then Zondi, a Zulu detective sergeant, appeared on the scene, as seemed only natural. I heard and saw and recorded what went on between them, before hurrying on to find out what would happen next.

Gradually, I became aware of various influences at work. Not long before, I had read *Cotton Comes to Harlem* by Chester Himes, and had been very impressed by how much I felt I'd learned about that particular society. Far more, I believed, than in any number of "worthier" works by James Baldwin and the like, who had obvious axes to grind. Then, by co-incidence, I'd heard Himes saying on television that he simply put everything down "the way it was," and I had been very impressed by that, too.

On further reflection, I realized that most of what I knew of different societies had came from a crime context. An uncle on my father's side, for instance, had been a judge at the Old Bailey, and this had led me to read the whole *Notable British Trials* series of transcripts. I doubt if there is a novel that can compare with, say, the trial of Sidney Fox for giving one a detailed picture of an English hotel chambermaid's life in the twenties. To think she hadn't considered it remarkable that old Mrs. Fox, ostensibly a member of the "idle rich," had worn six dresses at a time and smelled quite dreadful!

But most of all, I welcomed the *neutrality* of the crime story. Every novel about South Africa that I'd come across until then had been self-limiting, I felt, in that its antiapartheid slant made it appeal only to the "converted"—and this was essentially the reason I'd not been attracted by the form. Crime or mystery novels, on the other hand, appealed to pretty well everyone, including the more conservative, if not downright reactionary, reader. This meant I could simply write "the way it was" and leave people to make their own moral judgments while the *point* of the tale remained "who done it?" This seemed very much fairer—and ultimately, more valuable.

Two additional influences were also patently having an effect. One was the 87th Precinct stories of Ed McBain, to which I'd been introduced by a member of the dreaded se-curity police in South Africa. A certain terrifying officer had thrown *Like Love*, I think it was, at me and said: "Read it!" I'd done just that, being very surprised to find myself de-lighting in every word. McBain after McBain followed, and this, coupled with some novelist or another saying, "Write the sort of book you'd like to read yourself," gave me my basic approach.

On top of which, these long hours of television watching, which had so often made bearable an anxious, God-we're-broke evening, had convinced me of the very real worth of entertainment. First and foremost, I decided, my obligation was to entertain, leaving graver matters—which could be included, but obliquely—to those with the time, money, and intellectual capacity to indulge them.

I completed *The Steam Pig*, had it typed, and sent it off. Ten days later, as had been Anthony Price's experience, a Gollancz contract arrived. The chair had been sat in, found satisfactory, and bought! The advance didn't run to ja car, but I was able to buy a third-share in a converted lifeboat on the Thames.

Two books appeared that fall, both about the South Africa police and both based roughly on my hometown of Pieter-maritzburg. I had renamed it "Trekkersburg," and Tom Sharpe, who'd unbeknown to me written a black farce enti-tled *Riotous Assembly*, had called it "Piemburg."

Then the following February, *The Steam Pig* was chosen from an international short list as "The Best Crime Novel of 1971" and awarded the Crime Writers' Association Gold Dag-ger. What mattered most to me, however, was that while reviewers in South Africa greeted the *Pig* with parochial en-thusiasm, reviewers in other countries—notably Scandinavia and the United States—were finding it "a damning condem-nation of apartheid." This could only mean, I concluded, that people really had felt at liberty to make up their own minds about "the way it was," realizing my primary objective.

Much heartened, I began a second Kramer and Zondi mystery. I wrote a whole festoon of arresting first lines, but that's all they amounted to. I had to wait until I chanced on a theme that really made me indignant before *The Caterpillar*

Cop began to roll in the same intuitive fashion.

And this, I learned, was how Kramer and Zondi stories invariably came into being: they had to be based on issues which moved me deeply—just as the main theme of *The Steam Pig* had done. I also found that once this focus was established, I'd "forget it" and concentrate instead on the investigation, confident of an unconscious synthesis. "Psychologists have long been aware," Eric Bentley reminds us in his brilliant book, *The Life of the Drama*, "that the creative imagination, whether of scientists or artists, does not always work away at details and leave the discovery of an all-embracing unity till the end. It often starts out from unity vaguely apprehended and discovers details as it proceeds."

Tonight, I begin a new Kramer and Zondi novel. I've had this vague idea kicking about at the back of my mind for some time now: it will be the *first* K & Z story, and tell of how they originally joined forces in the early sixties. I've also this opening line, which has been waiting to prove useful for twelve years or more, "Like a cat she was quick and she slapped and the mosquito spread red on her thigh."

I'll see where I can get to. Chapter One is always the most difficult, and usually I rewrite it thirty times at least, trying to "get the tune right." My daughter Kirsty, a cellist, says what I'm really doing is trying to find the right *key* for the piece; it must be hell having a tone-deaf father who keeps insisting on making musical analogies. Like Ulysses Grant, you see, I can boast, "I know only two tunes, one's Yankee Doodle—and the other ain't." Sometimes I wonder whether writing, with its rhythms, loud and soft passages, fast and slow movements, isn't some form of compensatory activity on my part; I know I can tolerate almost any sound except music when I'm at the typewriter keyboard.

Three hours have gone by, and I have the first page written. The opening line is almost unchanged. The novel begins:

ONE

Like a cat she was quick, and her hand slapped and the mosquito spread red on her thigh.

"Fat mosquito," he said. "Whose blood?"

"Not mine," she said.

"Nor mine either."

They lay very still. The marsh frogs croaked. A crocodile splashed off a mud bank. Two owls gave their calls, one low and one high.

And I know, from how tense I am, from how many times I've got up to walk round the room, from how many pipes I've filled, half-smoked, filled again, from the way I briskly brush my palms together, Chapter One is rolling.

Back in the old days, when I wrote *The Steam Pig* and *The Caterpillar Cop*, there would be no rest for me now for the next fourteen days. Two weeks was the length of my *Oxford Mail* vacation, and because I feared I'd "lose the thread" once I was back at work, I'd make sure of reaching the last page before then. It was a headlong, head-swirling, dreamlike pounding that began at ten in the morning and went on, with breaks only to go to the bathroom, until four or five the next morning, day after day.

Then, when I was about to begin *The Gooseberry Fool*, my vacation was postponed. So I wrote it over seven weekends instead, with a final burst of nonstop typing that lasted from Friday evening until 7:30 P.M. on Sunday, when *Morecambe and Wise*, a favorite comedy show, was screened on television. I watched it, barely able to see or to hear properly, familiar side effects of fatigue by now, and stayed awake only by having yet another pint glass of Coca-Cola, which I rely on as some use coffee.

It wasn't simply I needed a laugh. It was also a form of tribute to the Morecambe and Wise double act, men of genius when it came to timing, an economy of words, vivid description, knowing just how to deliver a punchline. And today, now that I'm teaching writing, my first piece of advice for aspirant novelists is to listen to the greatest storytellers I know, stand-up comedians.

I've just broken off to take another crack at the first chapter of the new Kramer and Zondi novel, which now has *The Body Odour* as a working title. I don't write my novels in fourteen days any longer; there's been no need since I resigned as deputy editor in 1974 to write professionally. But I still try to work at the rate of a page—or 350 words—an hour, simply to sustain momentum. I'm going to rewrite it from the second page. Somewhere on that page, something is bothering me, I'm not sure what, but I've a "block" on the third.

I used to despair when I hit a "block," because it meant I lost hours and hours, trying to push the story on. Then, finally, I learned that a "block" indicated I'd gone wrong a little way back, and there was this smart-ass censor inside of me, putting everything on "hold" till I found it.

One draft, that's all I do, so that when I eventually type the last sentence of the story, it is ready to go to the publishers. Or *almost* ready, because I read through it one last time, retyping a page even if only one word needs alteration. Having a word processor now is a boon; once, you could hardly move in my workroom for crumpled sheets of paper.

I've found the mistake I made on page two. I'd given the woman a name; that distracts at this stage. I'll type it again from the top.

In doing so, I've discovered a new twist to the narrative that surprises me, and it's followed by a spontaneous remark from a character that makes me chuckle; odd, I don't feel that *I* invented either—they've "just happened." Now, I'm going to go back and type the page yet again, tightening it up. I can't go on until I've a sense, however spurious, of completion.

Discovery is a vital part of writing for me. I don't write an outline first, let alone a chapter-by-chapter breakdown. I did that once, and I ruined a very good idea, grinding to a halt on page thirty-one, beside myself with boredom.

And that's my main controlling factor: I dread boredom—my own, or my readers'. This is why I'll cut and cut, trimming every scene down to its bare essentials, even if this means ditching, say, a piece of description that has taken three hours to write. Sometimes I've overdone this, prompting kinder reviewers to say of *Snake* that my style had become too "elliptical."

Style. I wasn't at all sure quite what was meant by this, when I began writing. I knew a writer was supposed to have one, but, being at a loss to know how it was created, I simply opted for writing sentences that looked as if they belonged in a book—they tended to be longer than in newspapers!—and strove for clarity.

Glancing back at *The Steam Pig* now, I wince at some of the "tough" prose it contains, echoes of Mickey Spillane, et al., but note that even then my technique probably owed more to television and film than it did to anything else. And the book which has influenced me the most has been Eric Bentley's already-quoted *The Life of the Drama*. He says what are for me the most wonderfully sensible things—such as, "The formula of soap operas and Westerns is a sound one. If we don't spend our days and nights watching them, that should be only because we have other things to do. Possibly they would prove monotonous after a while, but possibly, like peanuts and cigarettes, they would not. Even on a TV screen violence in action and suspense in narrative can seldom fail to hold interest. The psychology is sound and each man is a human being—a specimen of human psychology—before he is a scholar or a gentleman."

The first time I became properly aware of style was when I switched from Kramer and Zondi to write *Rogue Eagle*, a spy thriller that won the Silver Dagger in 1976. Gone was the "soap opera" cross-cutting from one character to another, and in its place I had to sustain the narrative from one point of view for most of the time, like in a Paul Newman film. Gone, too, to a large degree, were the complications of writing three different languages—Afrikaans, Zulu, and Tamil—all in English, and the further complications of portraying a Zulu, say, speaking English and speaking Afrikaans, which involve subtle changes in word order. The tone was altered, as the chief protagonist, Finbar Buchanan, was a man wholly unlike either Kramer or Zondi, and this had to be conveyed by a new word choice and rhythm.

Rogue Eagle, incidentally, represents the closest I've ever come to being autobiographical. The major who sends Buchanan into the Maluti Mountains of Lesotho is very much a portrait of my father, who spent the war pursuing the Ossewabrandwag, and when I was eighteen, and had just left school, I rode a thousand miles through the Maluti meeting many of the people the book uses in slightly altered form. My Kramer and Zondi novels, although based on firsthand experience, aren't the same thing at all.

And when I came to begin the next in the series, *The Sunday Hangman*, I realized just how technically demanding Trekkersburg could be. It was, I felt, not unlike writing science fiction, in that I had to get across what amounted to a totally alien world, with its strange languages, customs, scenery, and laws.

I've reached a descriptive passage in my new manuscript and I'm fighting it. I find them harder than anything else, except where I'm able to recycle parts of an old poem of mine, as I did in *The Steam Pig*, for instance, when describing the port of Durban. Much of the difficulty I experience originates in a belief that for description to be effective, it must have almost the immediacy of a painting, something that can be taken in, whole, at a glance. This in turn means I must dare to use the very minimum to create an effect, and it isn't always easy to judge whether all I've done is to produce a pencil sketch.

No, it will probably do as it is, so I'll move on to a piece of reasoned thinking that must now be included. I won't do this in indirect speech. I haven't a "trained mind" that copes easily with arranging ideas in logical sequence, but a brain that tends to bite through everything as though it were a club sandwich, picking up the full flavor but finding difficulty in distinguishing the ingredients. Dialogue, that's the answer: "reality" allows it to be a lot messier, and anyway, if most of my readers tend to be unintellectual like myself, they'll find it easier to follow.

> *"And so," he said, "why pick on me, hey? Can't I have a kaffir to help me that's taller?"*

I've set *The Body Odour* aside, having this essay to complete. In a way, the enforced break comes as a relief—it's getting tougher and tougher, writing a Kramer and Zondi book.

Once, it was bad enough trying to ignore disheartening reviews, but now there are all these academic assessments to make one self-conscious. To be sure, it's immensely gratifying that at long last a serious intent has been recognized, but I often find it very difficult not to use a plot to reply to points raised—just as I'm tempted to try pulling out all the stops and seeing whether I can *really* boggle the professors' bloody minds, hey, as Kramer might put it.

There is a way round this, though. All I have to do is to take down an Ed McBain, a Joe Gores, a couple of Sjöwall and Wahlöö, a John D. MacDonald, a Chester Himes, and a John Ball. Then, having read them over a weekend, I don't hesitate: I just get typing, feeling I also have a story to tell.

Later, when all is done, that will be the time to check to see whether the story has other things to say. It should do;

I leave the space between the lines for that, and the responsibility for filling them to that shriveled, prunelike object, the McClure soul. But I won't really know, of course, till the reviews and, more importantly, the readers' letters come in. With any luck, they'll arrive from the United States, from Germany, Italy, Holland, Czechoslovakia, Hungary, Sweden, Denmark, Japan, and South Africa.

Or part of South Africa, I should say. Kramer and Zondi, in one sense possibly the best-known and best-liked Afrikaner and Zulu in the world, don't appear in translation in their fatherland. The nearest I've ever come to knowing how they are regarded by these sections of the community was in 1974, when I visited "Trekkersburg" and found the books had a cult status among the South African police there, who admitted to a sense of reflected glory.

"But indubitably, boss," Zondi might remark, "in general, our peoples know a mud pie when they see one."

What I Know about Writing Spenser Novels

by Robert B. Parker and Anne Ponder

As soon as I could afford it, I became self-employed. Because I want to stay that way, I don't care what people think of my books, as long as they continue to buy them. That's what I tell people when they ask about my work. Writing novels about Spenser is commercially satisfying, but writing is hard work and like a lot of other things that are difficult, it's worth doing. So, I do it as well as I can. I take it seriously.

Writing is one of the ordering principles in my day. The appeal of my daily activities, their prime charm, whether writing or pumping iron, is probably autonomy—and also, you don't have to scrape up a partner. The possibility that a writer may become isolated is a danger for a writer who does nothing else but write. Isolation can become detrimental. It's, I think, why so many writers end up writing either about the crisis of imagination in the writer's life or the per-

Anne Ponder, who worked with Robert B. Parker on this essay, is Associate Academic Dean at Guilford College, Greensboro, North Carolina. The essay is a substantial extension and revision of one that first appeared in *The Armchair Detective*, XVII (Fall, 1984), 341–48.

fidy of the academic world where they are in residence some-place, both of which get pretty boring after a while. I didn't write my first novel until I was almost forty, so I have all that experience. I have a large number of friends, most of whom are nonliterary and some of whom are not literate. Also, I play ball, and I hang out, but I do give some thought to the need to have actual contact. Self-employment has always appealed to me, and not only in my writing but in my exercise I'm self-employed; that means I can do what I want to when I want to, and that pleases me.

I started writing in November of 1971. I had just gotten tenure at Northwestern University, having just completed my Ph.D. I had written a dissertation on Chandler, Hammett, and Ross Macdonald, and I knew I could do what they did. *The Godwulf Manuscript* took me a while because I was new and it was the first thing that I tried and I went slow and I had to outline. Now a book takes me three to four months. The first one took me a year and a half. I finished it in March of 1973 and it was accepted by the first publisher I tried three weeks after I sent it in and I haven't had a rejection since. I started out emulating Chandler in that first book, maybe the first book and a half, because I was in my novitiate, and whenever I wasn't clear on what to do I would actively think about Chandler and what Marlowe would have done.

What I write comes out of what I know but otherwise the Ph.D. work had no direct influence on my skills as a writer. Chandler once said of Hammett that he lacked the sound of music beyond a distant hill; and if I have that, as Chandler did, it derives in part from all the reading on the way to the Ph.D.—*Gammer Gurton's Needle, Ralph Roister Doister*, etc.

That's all useful to me, however much fun I make of it, and I do make fun of it, and it deserves to be made fun of. But that mass of data which resided inescapably inside of me is useful because it gives density and allusion, to the extent that there is some, to the work. It does what Hammett couldn't. Hammett's very flat. There are people who see that as a mark of excellence. I see it as a loss, because you don't have to give up minimalism, and precision, and conciseness. Hammett was unable to do what I think Chandler was able to do. Chandler lost nothing in management of language, just as Faulkner didn't lose anything when he moved to a somewhat larger richness than Hemingway. I think that Faulkner is a much better writer than Hemingway and Chandler is a much better writer than Hammett. But all of us have learned to write from Hemingway and some of the things Hemingway did will never be done better, such as "The Big Two Hearted River." I would, if I could push the magic button, write more like Faulkner than I would like Hemingway, even though I probably write more like Hemingway than like Faulkner. But Faulkner had something I lack: genius. Nobody can write like Faulkner.

I no longer think about any writer, though, but me when I write. If I sound like another writer, I do or I don't. I don't emulate anyone anymore. The literary allusions are not studies, but I am conscious of mining various sources for titles. I take some from popular music and some from literary sources like Donne and Yeats. The titles are effortful; I look for them. The title from *Catskill Eagle* comes from "The Tryworks" chapter in *Moby Dick*. Usually I conceive the title early in the outlining and treatment process, before writing the book. *Mortal Stakes* was an exception. I came to that title late in the writing or maybe even afterward. I am currently about halfway through the next Spenser novel which was titled *The Eighth Shelf*, a reference to the Ciardi translation of Dante's *Inferno*, when I started it but which I have now titled *Taming A Seahorse*, from Browning's "My Last Duchess." The literary allusions in the book come unbidden, effortlessly, and that is probably because at one time I read so much so intensively.

It may be a confession of fault, but writing is not that intellectual an exercise. It is visceral rather than intellectual. It's like trying to hit a curve ball. I could discuss how it's done, but that doesn't render the experience. It's only how you would do it if you slowed it down and talked about it. I write dialogue by and large by imagining the people talking. That's not quite an accurate description, but it's the best I can do. There is no way to render that experience. Dialogue flows along very easily for me.

My books are seldom edited. Ordinarily what comes out of my typewriter goes. That is partly the condition of the publishing business—not many editors edit; most editors acquire. The copy editors take care of spelling and punctuation for me and sometimes they also pick up mistakes. The readership will edit you. If you get something wrong with a gun, something minute, the mail will tell you you've made a mistake. But I write out of an outline which has been developed out of a scenario, and I know what's going to happen. I try very hard to get the word right and I may make changes as I compose, stop, make a pencil change, X out, or start over, but essentially I do one draft. I don't believe that editing produces fiction; it only improves it. My artistic judgment is finished when the last pages leave my typewriter. After that it's art or it's not and whatever else happens to it—selling any copies or not, made into a movie or not, featured on the front page of the *Times* or not—is all "spillikins in the parlor." It was art when I stopped typing it and after that it becomes a piece of commercial matter and we try to sell it.

What I put into the books includes what I've read, what I've experienced, and what I'm interested in. On one level at least, I write because it's what I can do. I suspect it's got something to do with my interest in autonomy but if so, the impulse is unconscious; and then, by definition, I don't understand it because if I did it wouldn't be unconscious.

Obviously, all of the things that people write—me, Homer, Mickey Spillane, Harold Robbins, whatever range you want— are written by people who have an unconscious and who have particular needs and who gratify them in ways they are aware of and in ways they are not. And while I don't think that one can decide, nor do I think literature is merely the pro- jection of unconscious needs, there may be things in myself that make possible the impossible various attempts at artistic execution. Certainly it is silly to pretend that writing is all a matter of artistic choice. Fitzgerald was writing about Zelda, at least in part, when he wrote *The Great Gatsby*, and John Updike could not have written *Rabbit Is Rich* thirty years ago. These things come out of one's self.

It is similarly impossible to be precise about my interior sources for the Spenser novels, but that's the question I get asked most often. How much is Spenser me and how much isn't he? I have no answer for that, but he comes out of me. Those are the most interesting questions about literature, though. How much of Joyce is in *The Portrait of an Artist*? Is that Joyce's boyhood or isn't it? I bet Joyce didn't know either. But perhaps Spenser is a commentary or an illumi- nated manuscript of me. I started the first book, *The Godwulf Manuscript*, when I was not yet forty. In fact, I had just turned thirty-nine and I am now fifty-three, so I am somewhat older. My children, in 1971, would have been twelve and eight. We have grown up together and learned a great deal. I have been with Joan Parker for those additional years and I have learned much from her and I know I have changed and grown and enlarged—no physical humor here, friends— over the years. I have come more and more to understand complexity and difficulty—more and more to achieve flex- ibility. I've been getting calmer and calmer about life and its grotesqueries.

The relationship between men and women and the rela- tionship between fathers and sons has been the paramount interest of my life and remains so. Those concerns naturally grow into my work. For entirely unliterary reasons, but also for literary economy, I write about what I can write about. That's an amazingly difficult concept for beginning writers to grasp, but it's the cliché of every writing class—"to write about what you know." I draw on what I know and what I care about and what I know and care about most is parent/child relationships and husband/wife relationships, and I think that, more than any intellectual or literary impulse, sustains Spenser's character. Spenser can't save the world he's in, because it's not a controllable, self-contained place, but he makes choices about what he will and will not do. Some of Spenser's choices put him in the role of detective as parent. Spenser's relationship to Kevin Bartlett in *God Save the Child* and to Paul Giacomin in *Early Autumn* are two examples. Spenser cares about people who are in need of help. He is also a detective as savior of maidens. I have no desire to offend feminist critics, but women and children are better objects for salvation by a male hero than are other men. Women are less powerful still and children are classically powerless. Spenser's commitment is less, I think, to children and women than it is to the powerless. Women and children serve as a nice metaphor for the powerless. I also do know about children; I have two, and I have the good fortune to be their father. I'd much rather be their father than be Spenser's creator. I'd much rather be married to Joan Parker than be a writer.

But beyond my experience with women and children, the unspoken and inarticulate love relationship between Spenser and Hawk and to a lesser extent between Spenser and a number of other characters (including the bad guys who are beloved adversaries in some ways like the lions in Hemingway) comes out of my experiences with men in groups. I know a lot about locker rooms and gyms. I've talked to a lot of cops since I've been a writer and most of the cops tell me that I've got it about right. They're not talking about police procedure; they're talking about what it's like being a cop. Well, I've never been a cop, but I've been with people who might be cops. I've been in the army and I've been on athletic teams. I've been in locker rooms and gyms and I know what those guys are like. Part of me is like that too. I still play ball in a twilight league with uniforms and umpires and lights and team jackets. Mine says "Bob–1" on the sleeve. My batting average is going down in inverse proportion to my age.

In the books the games and sports serve the function of a couple of clowns in Shakespeare who stand on stage and say, "Look at that wedding going on," or to fill time while Hal goes from England to France and back the characters say, "Look at that battle raging." When the grim necessity of exposition periodically intrudes, as it must even in the most crafty of prose—the cooking and the dining in particular, but also the weight-lifting and hitting the bag—all make for wonderful stage business. In fact, most people don't even know they're getting dosed with exposition, because they are looking at Hawk and Spenser doing a little tune on the light bag, but in the process of that the reader learns something. I don't remember what, because I don't remember which book they do that in. The books fade for me. They're all one long story. But it softens the red-neck outlines for Spenser to cook or for him to read. It's perfectly appropriate for a guy who lives alone; he reads. Those literary allusions, the cooking, tell us a little about him and they also give me something to do while I'm letting you know that somebody's put out a contract on somebody.

The games and occupations are important. They do define who and what Spenser is. The physicality is after all an appropriate part of what he does; it tells you a little bit about the kind of guy he is. It's also handy. If you're gonna do Spenser's job, you probably ought to be big and strong. I use games, the running, the weight-lifting to flesh out character and to disguise exposition, but they are important for another reason. It has been said that "life is fatal, but not serious." On a large scale that's a definition of all sports. Sport is a creation of rules and the consequences are exciting, but they can't really matter. Who won the World Series two years ago, real quick? I don't remember. Also, in a random universe, sports matter because they are, if you accept the premise, entirely self-contained. It works. Nobody ever argues that three strikes shouldn't be out. They may argue if it's a third strike or not, but no one says, "Wait a minute, I want four strikes." It's an entirely stable universe in its context. All of those things are also accomplishment oriented. They do something. If you can bench-press 250 pounds or 300 pounds, how many times can you do it? That's a definable result and it also shows up. You get very big pectoral muscles and a fine-looking thick neck like mine.

Cooking, too, has its own intrinsic order. They're all ordering techniques, but they're also ways of talking about Spenser. In his attempts to impose upon chaos a certain amount of order, he does everything in an orderly fashion. If he does it, he tries to do it right. He dresses appropriate to the occasion and is careful that his clothes fit. If he's going to cook, he doesn't boil an egg; he cooks. If he goes out to eat, if he can he tries to eat a satisfying and well-done meal. He tries to cook and eat as well as he can. He tries to keep himself in shape as well as he can. All of that is at work.

As I have gotten older, Spenser has gotten older. I am a writer who certainly makes maximum use of his own life experiences. On the other hand, neither of my sons was ever particularly like Paul Giacomin. The ordinary circumstantial realism is drawn when possible from things which I can talk about. I lift weights; Spenser lifts weights. I run; he runs. If I did needlepoint, he'd do needlepoint, but I don't. If I played chess, he'd play chess, but I don't. I've tried to teach him, but he's not smart enough to learn.

No writer can transmit experience into fiction without filtering it through imagination, however direct that transmission may be. The simplistic biographical questions like "How much like Susan Silverman is Joan Parker?" and "Is your son the dancer just like Paul Giacomin?" and "Is Rachel Wallace a sympathetic Marilyn French?" are almost offensive to a writer because he's being accused of just recycling his life. I've never met Marilyn French, for instance, or read her book. I know her name, period. One of my early fan letters said that the villain in *The Godwulf Manuscript* was very clearly John Gardner and there was no way I could deny it, and what did I have to say about that? I wrote back saying, "You leave me few options." In fact, I had not laid eyes on Gardner nor read any of his books. I have since. Before he died I met him and he looked not unlike the character, but there was no biography in that. Susan Silverman is more accurately described as my taking my reaction to Joan Parker and giving it to Spenser. Susan is more limited than Joan Parker. Joan Parker is a little better looking than Susan. Joan Parker is not Jewish. Some of that I do on purpose so that I'm not too close to the subject matter. Obviously, it is not inane to speculate about a correspondence between Joan and Susan, but what that relationship is in detail is beyond my powers to say. James said it matters not so much what experience you have, it's what you do with it. I have never been a detective, I have never been a professional boxer, I have never been down and out in California as Boone Adams is in *Love and Glory*. Even though *Three Weeks in Spring* is an autobiographical, factual rendition of things that happened to Joan and me, it is transmuted through imagination and organized and modified and colored. Stripped of its nineteenth-century elegance, James's essay on "The Art of Fiction" is as useful as I know and better than I can do in describing that indescribable process.

That brings me to another point: I don't think of myself as writing detective fiction. Other than the fact that the protagonist of the Spenser books is a detective, I have very little in common with other people who write detective stories. The things that connect me with Agatha Christie are a lot less significant than the things which separate me. Even in the beginning the books were never about who took the Maltese falcon or what happened to the Brasher doubloon. Crime and its solution or even crime and punishment are not the central issues. Spenser is more and more interested in matters of the human behavior (such as honor and love) and steadily less interested in the conventional metier of detective fiction. In each book there is some matter of mortal significance and that is what justifies what might be considered ethically realistic behavior patterns on Spenser's part. The stakes are mortal and a person can prevail insofar as he or she is not finally overwhelmed by a corrupt world.

I have come to notice that the center probably does not hold, but there's nothing much I can do about it. What we know is that life—your life, my life, everybody's life—will eventually discorporate. It seems to me that the ratio between joy and suffering is unfortunately balanced. The disordered world we face was not discovered by Yeats in the early part of the century. Voltaire even noticed it. It's right that the center doesn't hold, and that you can't make it hold. But you should try to make it hold. That's the pleasure in it. I am interested (and I suspect that the people who read my books are interested) in the image of a hero who is self-disciplined, reasonably autonomous, and able to control his fear of death and his desire for sex and money. In that image, like the image of the Western hero or the image of the Arthurian knight, the reader finds some consolation, some temporary stay against confusion.

What I write more nearly resembles a Western than it does other detective novels. I am certainly more like A. B. Guthrie than like Agatha Christie. I subscribe to much that Robert

Warshow said in *The Westerner*. (The Western in its pure form is not flourishing in literature these days and I couldn't write one; it would take too much research. Since I grew up in western Massachusetts, even horses are foreign to my experience. But with a film-star cowboy as president, if culture produces art there ought to be some good Western books written and Western films made.)

Warshow said that the Western is the last art form that gives serious consideration to questions of honor and violence. The crucial point in the Western is not when the Westerner will draw his gun but when he won't. The point in a classic Western like *Shane* or *High Noon* is that the gun gets drawn when appropriate, rather than randomly. Where Western movies began to descend and lose their grip was when filmmakers didn't understand that or chose to demythify it, like Peckinpah's *The Wild Bunch* demythified *Shane* by substituting nostalgia and camaraderie of men in groups. The violence in the Spenser novels shares the view of the classic Western. The fact that Spenser will kill somebody is much less significant than the fact that he won't or that he does so in a controlled, almost civilized fashion. Like Shane, Spenser kills when he must. *Shane* is, in many ways, about how a hero won't kill until he must, and when he must, he does. It is not random. It is done with reason. I don't know of any other art form at the moment than the kind of books I write which considers violence as controllable, necessary, and subject to a code of behavior. The bad guys in my books will do anything, but Spenser is what Warshow calls "the last gentleman."

Like the Westerner, the significant conflict for Spenser comes "...when his moral code, without ceasing to be compelling, is seen also to be imperfect. The Westerner at his best exhibits a moral ambiguity which darkens his image and saves him from absurdity; this ambiguity arises from the fact that, whatever his justifications, he is a killer of men." The same Spenser who couldn't or wouldn't shoot Harry Cotton in *Early Autumn* gets sick after he kills Leo the pimp in *Catskill Eagle*, but he shoots Jerry Costigan without hesitation. These novels are about how a man without extraordinary prestige or wealth behaves honorably. Such a character is, by definition, heroic. I do refer to some mythic patterns. For example, Spenser is a man without parents. In *Catskill Eagle* he reveals the circumstances of his birth and childhood and he fits the pattern in which the hero emerges spontaneously rather than from a traditional lineage.

Since the mythology of the Western is inhospitable to complex, interesting female characters, Spenser's world clearly exceeds the Western formula because it is inhabited by women like Susan Silverman, Linda Rabb, Rachel Wallace, Brenda Loring, and Cindy Sloan. They understand the themes important to Spenser—honor and integrity and autonomy—and one of the reasons these women are interesting is that they understand him so well. The reader also perceives Spenser as better than he might otherwise be perceived because these good women do understand him and they explain this understanding to him.

Spenser can't wholly understand himself in the context of the culture in which he moves, that is, among other men. He struggles least in a male bonding atmosphere in which much is done but little is said. Women represent societal views in the Western but, as Warshow points out, the Westerner finally represents the deeper wisdom. The women, not because they are female, but because they represent society in the movies, are shown to be naive. For instance, Gracy Kelly in *High Noon* is a classic example of a sappy woman who finally learns real values by shooting a guy. Some critics have trouble with that, but if you deal with it at the mythic level it confirms what Leslie Fiedler suggests, that civilization is the threat and that an isolated man who lives outside of civilization, Huck honey, and imposes his own code, is wiser and less corrupt. I'm writing, at least in part, at that mythic level and not always consciously.

However, in my books, the relationships between the women and Spenser are progressively more substantial than the relationship between Miss Kitty and Matt Dillon in *Gunsmoke*. I'm perfectly capable of writing about and presenting an adult, intelligent, full-fledged female character as fully fleshed out as I can a male character within the limits of my not being a woman. Joan Parker understands my books and me in a way that no one else does. She's not able to read my books as novels because we've known each other too intimately and too long, but she likes them better as the women characters have become more fully articulated and less adjunct to the hero. I think that her influence on me has made that more possible as the years have gone by.

Even with what she has taught me, the limitation is a real one. I know all that stuff about you-don't-have-to-be-a-cook-to-know-a-bad-soufflé, but I cannot write from a female point of view because I think there's sufficient difference between my experience and a woman's so that it would be a little artificial. I have been asked if I'm ever going to write a book about Hawk, to which I say the same thing, No, that's all I know about Hawk. I couldn't do that, either.

However, Hawk is an increasingly important character in the Spenser novels. He and Spenser work together through almost all of *Catskill Eagle*, which is the longest book I have written. In it both Hawk and Spenser, a dynamic duo, rescue Susan Silverman. I've never been interested in plot, except that you need some to get the story told. I am not in any way conscious of an overall structure like a revenge structure or rescue structure (except in retrospect I can see both at work in *Catskill Eagle*) nor am I thinking ahead to the next book. When I began to write *Taming a Seahorse*, I came to it six months after having completed *Catskill Eagle*. I gave no thought to *Catskill Eagle* other than not to contradict it. As in life, what happens in previous years influences what happens in later years.

I do use the history of the characters in the series, and not many writers do, except Faulkner and me. Spenser has a history, and it weighs on him as it does on humans, and what he does grows out of what he did, and that will continue to be so. The history of the characters develops as the reader discovers that it exists. There is more of Spenser's fictional history in the recent books because in the early books there was less of it to use. I'm not aiming toward finding a culmination in which Spenser represents my vision of mankind and humanity itself. I'm just doing a book at a time. And I build on what I've done because of the same kind of literary economy that I build on what I personally do. I used what happened in *Savage Place* in *Valediction* and references to *Looking for Rachel Wallace* and *Judas Goat* in *Catskill Eagle*.

Hawk and Susan Silverman and Martin Quirk and Paul Giacomin and Rachel Wallace and Hugh Dixon reappear because they are the characters in Spenser's fictional history, and each of these characters also has a history. My characters never do anything that surprises me. I make them all up. I try to make them consistent with the characters I've vested them with, but they do not have a life of their own, except to speak metaphorically. For example, I had no intention in putting Hugh Dixon in *Catskill Eagle* other than to make use of him in the plot. I have no idea whether I will use him again. I had no idea that I was writing a rescue structure, and I had no intention in using Rachel Wallace other than that she seemed appropriate. Perhaps at some level below the surface of my literary consciousness her appropriateness may be connected to the rescue motif.

Whether all of that is critically defensible doesn't concern me; *Catskill Eagle* is a best-seller. I would prefer that everyone like my books rather than dislike them, but I'd rather have everyone buy them than either like them or dislike them. I do this for a living.

Life is scarily good. My marriage is idyllic; the children are grown and they have good lives. I got an amazing amount of control (for a writer) consulting with producer John Wilder on a Spenser television movie. My books are selling in great numbers. I work out on the Nautilis and weigh two hundred twenty pounds, which isn't nearly as bad as it could be. I'm in pretty good shape; my back doesn't hurt. I am in considerable demand in the marketplace. I feel wanted. I'm proud of the writing. I care about each book very much, and I make it as good as I can make it. And I don't care what anyone thinks about it very much beyond that. The work satisfies me, and if it doesn't satisfy me, I am satisfied that I can't do it better. I'm an apostle of the possible.

Afterword

Reading essays like these can be instructive, entertaining, humbling. For a reviewer—I hesitate to say critic—of mystery fiction, mostly humbling. These writers know how to do the short sentence. They also, as nearly all of them say, really don't pay much attention to what the critics (or the reviewers) say. Or so they tell us. I do notice that they must have read some reviews, at least, for there are any number of corrections of my reviews cunningly wedged into these essays. So, for the record, let me report, not the differences of opinion but the clear corrections of fact:

I once suggested in a review that Reginald Hill just might also be Jack S. Scott, my antennae all aflap for similarities of style and plot. Reginald Hill wrote to me on the day he sent in his essay, as a P.P.S. (never mind the P.S.), "I am not, never have been, nor is it my present intention ever to be, Jack Scott!" That exclamation mark says a lot.

Then there was that review in which I cleverly identified Tony Hillerman's capitol reporter with Springfield, Illinois, and he has waited until now to tell me that I can't tell Oklahoma City from my elbow.

Or Robert Barnard, to whom I put questions based on surmises in earlier reviews: why Dickens (his scholarly field)? why Leeds (where he lives)? "Why not?" he said to the Dickens question, and on second thought I decided no one really need account for an interest in Dickens. "Because it has an opera company," he said to the second question, and I thought about how I was editing this collection, and writing this note, in Santa Fe, New Mexico, partially because it had an opera company. Perhaps we tribe of reviewers look a bit too hard, and forget the main purpose of the literature we are peering down upon so intensely through our magnifying glass: to entertain. Hillerman's most difficult writing assignment, though he doesn't admit to it in his essay, was to compose eighteen different Purina Pig Chow radio commercials every week. Now that's entertainment.

Robin W. Winks

The Contributors

Robert Barnard's novels include *Corpse in a Gilded Cage, Out of the Blackout, Fête Fatale*, and *Death and the Princess*. *Political Suicide* and *Bodies* are scheduled for publication in 1986. He lives in Leeds, England.

Rex Burns won the Edgar in 1976 for *The Alvarez Journal*. Other recent novels include *The Avenging Angel, Strip Search*, and *Ground Money* (forthcoming). He lives in Colorado.

K. C. Constantine is a pseudonym for the author of the Mario Balzic novels, including *Always a Body to Trade, The Man Who Liked Slow Tomatoes*, and *A Fix Like This*.

Dorothy Salisbury Davis, Grand Master of the Mystery Writers of America, will publish her twentieth novel, *The Habit of Fear*. Other recent novels include *Lullaby of Murder, Scarlet Night*, and *A Death in the Life*. She lives near New York City.

Michael Gilbert, a solicitor by training, has published more than twenty novels with the Inspector Hazelrigg series character. Recent novels include *The Black Seraphim, The Final Throw*, and *Death of a Favourite Girl*. He lives in Kent, England.

Donald Hamilton, author of more than twenty-five Matt Helm novels, lives in Santa Fe, New Mexico. Some recent books include *The Annihilators, The Revengers*, and *The Mona Intercept*.

207

Joseph Hansen publishes under his own name and also as James Colton and Rose Brock. Recent Hansen books include *Steps Going Down, Brandstetter and Others*, and *Nightwork*. He lives in Los Angeles.

Tony Hillerman's novels, set on a Navajo Indian reservation, feature Sergeant Jim Chee or Lieutenant Joe Leaphorn. Recent novels include *The Ghostway, The Dark Wind*, and *People of Darkness*. He lives in Santa Fe, New Mexico.

Reginald Hill features Superintendent Andrew Dalziel in his novels. Recent books include *Exit Lines, Deadheads, Traitor's Blood*, and *Who Guards a Prince?* He also writes under the names Dick Morland, Patrick Ruell, and Charles Underhill. He lives in Yorkshire, England.

James McClure was born in South Africa but now lives in Oxford, England. Recent novels include *The Artful Egg, The Blood of an Englishman*, and *The Sunday Hangman*. His series characters are Lieutenant Kramer and Sergeant Zondi.

Robert B. Parker wrote his first Spenser novel in 1973. Recent Spenser novels include *A Catskill Eagle, Valediction*, and *The Widening Gyre*. He lives near Boston.

Anne Ponder is Associate Academic Dean at Guilford College in Greensboro, North Carolina.

Robin W. Winks is the Randolph W. Townsend Jr. Professor of History at Yale University. The author of many books, including *Detective Fiction* and *Modus Operandi*, he also reviews mysteries for the Boston *Globe* and other publications. He lives in Connecticut.

Index